FORGIVE, FORGET AND BE FREE

JEANETTE LOCKERBIE

FORGIVE, FORGET AND BE FREE
by Jeanette Lockerbie

Published by
HERE'S LIFE PUBLISHERS, INC.
P.O. Box 1576
San Bernardino, California 92402

ISBN 0-89840-068-6
Library of Congress Catalog Card 84-048100
HLP Product Number 950782

Unless otherwise noted, Scripture quotations are from The New American Standard Bible, © The Lockman Foundation, 1960, 1962, 1963, 1968, 1971, 1972, 1973, 1975, and are used by permission.

Other Scripture quotations are from the King James Version (KJV), the Berkeley translation, the Revised Standard Version (RSV), The Living Bible (TLB), and the New English Bible (NEB). The author acknowledges with appreciation permission to quote from: *Tomorrow's At My Door,* by Jeanette Lockerbie, Fleming H. Revell, © 1973.

Contents

Foreword

When Jeanette Lockerbie writes a book, it is always special.

It is special because she is a professional writer and conveys her message clearly to the reader.

It is special because she anchors her writing to the Eternal Word of God. She doesn't wander around, but rather screens her ideas throughout the pages of the Bible.

It is special because it has to do with everyday living. Jeanette writes about here and now—problems and concerns.

It is special because it speaks to everyone and deals with insightful, biblical answers to the problem of forgiveness.

I trust this book will be special to you, and lift you to greater heights in your Christian walk.

Clyde M. Narramore

Acknowledgments

First, to my daughter Jeannie Lockerbie and her colleague Lynn Silvernale for supplying their thoughtful and scriptural concepts on forgiveness.

To Mrs. Sharon Segress for her part in typing much of the manuscript.

To Dr. Clyde Narramore for his ongoing encouragement and support.

To the many people who have spoken freely of their trauma and difficulty in the area of forgiveness and who have granted me permission to retell their experiences. (All names and identifying circumstances have been changed to protect their identities.)

To the Narramore Christian Foundation for permission to quote from articles by Dr. Jeanette Acrea and Dr. George Martindale. These articles appeared in the foundation's publication, *Psychology for Living*.

Finally, to all on the staff of Here's Life Publishers who have any part in the publication of this book, my warm thanks.

Introduction

For some years I have emphasized the importance of a forgiving spirit. Sometimes the reaction has been, "You wouldn't say that if you knew how badly I've been treated." At other times there have been all kinds of justification that "my case is different; God doesn't mean me; I do forgive but the other person keeps on with the same behavior." Almost always there has been the self-defeating, "I can't forgive *myself.*"

Along the way the Lord has had to teach me — often the hard way — how to forgive and, as much as is humanly possible, forget. *And nothing is more liberating.*

Forgiveness is a form of giving, maybe the highest form.

Forgiveness is a gift we give ourselves, initially through being able to appropriate God's forgiveness. Then, through the heavenly economics that "It is more blessed to give than to receive," we are twice blessed, as we exercise forgiveness toward one another.

Forgiveness is an investment that brings guaranteed dividends: "As we forgive..." we are forgiven: measure for measure.

A forgiving spirit keeps us close to God; we keep short accounts with Him. Rather than feed on resentment and bitterness, a forgiving spirit enables us to direct our energy toward the reconciling of God's people to one another.

On the physical and emotional levels, the personal benefits of being a forgiving person are great. Just one of these is a reduction of tension and hostility, which often are contributors to depression. Also, the ability to put everyday slights and hurts into a true, eternal perspective keeps one on a more even keel. Likewise, since "forgive" is a command from God, by our very obedience to His Word,

7

we put ourselves in line for the blessings which accrue to those who are obedient.

On the minus side, the people whom we will not forgive will haunt our prayer life. We will, in a sense, always be chained to them. By not forgiving them we are handing to them a measure of control over our thought life, and "As a man thinks, so is he," the Bible tells us.

Finally, we should be motivated to forgive *because God has forgiven us,* and He keeps on forgiving us. Being the recipient of *so great* forgiveness, in unlimited measure, we can afford to be generous in forgiving others.

To help you work toward genuine forgiveness in a systematic way, I have prepared some questions for you to think about. You will find them at the end of the book. These also could be used by a discussion group desiring to grow in the area of forgiveness.

It's my earnest prayer that, as you read this book and consider anew its mighty theme, God will bless and enrich your life as He has blessed me while teaching me how to forgive. It's often a difficult journey, but in the end a glorious one.

Jeanette Lockerbie
Pasadena, California

1
You Can't Mean It, God

When your memories hold more resentment than thanksgiving, you're in trouble.

MUST WE ALWAYS forgive?

Is there never an exception?

Florence insists "I can't — I *won't* forgive my husband. I don't see how You would want me to forgive him, God. For twenty years I've loved him and been faithful to him. Now this...." She wrung her hands in an agony of grief. "No! I can never forgive him for this heartache and humiliation."

Relentless hatred and bitterness toward her husband and the other woman began to eat at her, fed on such thoughts as, *People are talking, saying I'm to blame and I'm just getting what I deserve. And some are pitying me. That's even worse.* So she walked with her head high — and an empty heart. All the while she kept telling herself, *Even God in heaven would never expect me to forgive my husband.*

On the other hand, note Joyce's reaction.

Arriving home one afternoon from a pleasant lunch with

some church friends, she found a note propped by the telephone. "What's this?" she said with a warm smile. "Vince and his little notes. What message is he giving me this time? 'Pick up my suit at the cleaners'? 'Call your mother before six'?" But no. She glanced at the note, then dropped it as though it would burn her. "No. NO," she screamed. "No, Vince, I don't believe it." She stopped and picked up the note as if reading it a second time would change what it said. But there it was in Vince's funny, undeniable writing. "I'm leaving you, Joyce. I've found someone else. Don't try to change my mind. This is final. My attorney will get in touch with you. Vince."

Joyce slumped into the nearest chair, feeling she would never recover from this sudden blow. And the farthest thing from her mind was forgiving her husband. "How can I *ever* forgive him, Lord," she moaned. "Even You would not expect that of me."

Two women with the same problem and the same initial reaction to it.

What made the difference in the outcome for Joyce?

Unlike Florence, she did not continue to feed her bitter feelings, did not nurture her understandable hurt and resentment. Rather, after initially reeling from the blow, Joyce began to analyze the situation as best she could. Along the way she concluded that it takes two to create a problem. She then asked the Lord to show her where she had failed. As she continued to read her Bible and spend time with the Lord, she began to realize, *I'll never have peace of heart until I can forgive Vince, hard though that will be.*

But the day came when with glowing face, she related to me, "I'll never forget the very hour when, on my knees, I found myself praying not only for Vince but for the woman who had so hurt me and who was now Vince's wife." As though she thought I didn't believe what she was saying, she added, "I really did, or, rather the Holy Spirit within me enabled me to forgive them. I also asked the Lord to forgive me for my wrong feelings about Him. It was like being liberated from a chain that was binding me."

Joyce need not have tried so hard to convince me of her

10

sincerity. I can look back in my own life and pinpoint a time when God gave me such strength and grace, and I was able to forgive. And the joyous part is that the very people whom I had said I could never forgive—"God, You wouldn't expect me to"—are now among my best friends. This is one of the pluses of obedience. God does expect us to have a forgiving spirit, and to activate it, *whatever the circumstances.* In turn, He rewards our obedience with joy unspeakable. I have found this to be true.

Reclaiming the Years

I was revisiting a town where I had once lived. My hostess, Edith, was a woman I had not seen or heard from in many years. We had a lot of catching up to do. She had been widowed, and something about her was different— her spirit—she had become hard and calloused.

Sitting by her fireside while drinking innumerable cups of tea, we became reacquainted. Each morning we read the Bible together and prayed. But she said never a word about her church. That is, until the afternoon we were out walking and passed a beautiful stone house. I remarked on the architecture and she said, "That's the parsonage." A few more minutes brought us to a church, and I paused to read the bulletin board. When I inquired about the minister, Edith seemed to stiffen. "He's a new minister," was all she volunteered.

Later that evening I broached the subject of the church I had seen. "You haven't told me much about your church yet, Edith." Her warm smile vanished; she set her lips in a hard, straight line that spoiled her sweet appearance.

"I don't go," she replied, "I haven't gone for *seven years.*"

She waited for my reaction, and when I made no comment she continued, "The day I buried my husband— seven years ago—the minister said to me, 'I'll be around to see you,' but he never came. And I'll *never forgive* him. How could I be expected to?" She looked into the glowing coals as though seeing bygone days, then in a bitter tone added, "So I just stay away from his church. I've never been back since then."

11

What could I say?

I tried to draw her out, to get her to talk more about it: "But have you not missed being at church, Edith?"

"Oh, yes," she admitted, "I still miss it. I miss the singing, I miss chatting with my old friends after the service, and — yes — I miss the sermon, too." Her voice had softened but now it grew hard again. With a defiant toss of her head she said, "Why should I go when the minister didn't keep his word? Aren't ministers of the gospel *always* supposed to keep their word?"

It was no time to go into a defense of ministers. And, without a doubt, from what she told me, this widow had a just grievance. With a quick prayer for the right words, I asked softly, "Didn't you mention that there's a new minister now?"

"I'll go make more tea," was her way of dismissing the subject.

I was concerned for her. She needed her church. She needed to get rid of the cords of bitterness that were binding her. She needed to stop cheating herself of the peace of heart that comes with being right with God and other people. I began to pray for her, and for myself that the Lord might use me in some way in answering my prayer for her. The following day when she appeared to be in a mellow mood, I suggested, "Edith, I've been thinking — maybe you would consider giving the new minister a chance. Who knows? Maybe he's not aware of what happened seven years ago. And anyway" — I got bolder — "I think it will make you feel better yourself, so I would like you to seriously consider forgetting the past and going back to your church. Of course it won't be easy, but, if you make that step in faith you can do it in the power of the Holy Spirit."

Two days later, she accompanied me to the airport bus terminal. And just before we parted she said almost in a whisper, "Jeanette, I've thought over what you said. It'll be hard — but *I'm going back to my church.*"

I hugged her and said, "You've made me very happy, Edith."

I could leave, confident that the winter in her heart had

started to thaw: where before it had been "his" church, now it was "my" church.

I've heard from Edith since then, and from what she writes I know she is learning the wonderful truth of Joel 2:25, *"And I will restore to you the years that the locust hath eaten"* (KJV).

When we are willing to extend forgiveness and let bygones be bygones, the Lord allows us to recapture the time that was lost.

But *must* we always forgive?

This is a question we can quite reasonably raise. But how to answer it?

There are some — among them respected theologians — who would tell us that no, we do not always have to forgive; only when the conditions are right. They may cite their proof texts and outline biblical provisions for forgiveness. However, I side with those theologians who believe that it is always in order to have a forgiving spirit.

For what reasons?

One: obedience. "Be ye kind to another...*forgiving one another"* (Ephesians 4:32 KJV) is not a suggestion but a scriptural directive.

Two: because God *for Christ's sake* has forgiven me.

Three: forgiving is a *privilege.* Christ has committed to me the ministry of reconciliation (2 Corinthians 5:19).

Now, how do we proceed?

The first step must always be *accepting responsibility for dealing with the situation* that calls for forgiving.

Then, *pray* for "them which despitefully use you, and persecute you" (Matthew 5:44 KJV).

Next, *go to the person.*

We go to the person for his good, as well as to restore our own peace of mind. Ideally, healing will take place. Another reason to go to the individual is that he may not even be aware of having caused any hurt: not all such incidents are with malice aforethought. You may get this response, "I didn't realize I'd done that. Thanks for coming and telling me, and please forgive me."

Obviously, in such an instance, we have in mind lesser hurts, not the kind that devastate and have a lasting effect

13

on one's life.

The Lord provides two other opportunities for the offender. In each of these also, you are the one who must take the initiative; taking along one or two people in the hope that their input will help, and in order that they may be witnesses to what is said. If this measure fails to cause the person to repent, you have the backing of Scripture to bring the matter to the church (many Bible teachers interpret "the church" as the *church leaders*, not the open congregation).

If the person still resists all efforts, yours and the church's, to repent and make things right, the responsibility it no longer yours. You have obeyed the teaching of the Bible, and, as I mentioned earlier, obedience has its own rewards. But, because you are human, you may find a certain smugness creeping in: "There, I've done everything *I* should do, the rest is up to him." You will never be discharged of the obligation to *pray* for the one who has sinned against you, even though you have forgiven the person.

Sylvia went to her pastor for some counsel as to how she could deal with a problem involving her stepmother. The pastor outlined the scriptural steps, but Sylvia countered with, "But, Pastor, I am the injured party. Doesn't that make a difference? Must I be the one to ask for forgiveness?"

"If you want to have peace, Sylvia, you'll have to go God's way. The responsibility is on you, for you are the Christian. And you'll be glad you did," he encouraged her.

"I'll think about what you've told me," she promised. "Maybe the right time will come for me to do it." (One of Satan's snares is to keep us thinking, *When the right opportunity presents itself,* or *I'll wait for the right moment.* You'll have to make both time and opportunity; they will never just "come.")

Dredging Up the Past

One of the very real hindrances to clearing up difficulties between people is letting your mind dwell on past wrongs they have done to you. When you become aware of such thoughts, simply refuse to give them more than momentary attention. It's a matter of "You can't prevent the birds from flying overhead, but you *can* keep them from nesting in your hair." Dredging up past hurts — when the situation has been scripturally dealt with and should be forgotten — can only hinder your spiritual growth and keep you emotionally burdened.

If you find yourself continually dwelling on faults and sins, try dwelling on how many of yours God has forgiven and blotted out. Nancy had experienced difficulty in putting away negative thoughts and feelings about a fellow church member who had brought much grief into her life. "Then one day," Nancy related, "I caught a glimpse of myself as God must see me. A real look at what *I* am apart from the ongoing grace of God to me. The old feelings and thoughts left me and have never returned."

Another way to make forgiveness a reality is to take some positive steps in the direction of the one you have forgiven. Debbie told me her experience: "Linda and I had been good friends until she turned on me and made a heap of problems for me. It was hard for me to forgive her — but I realized forgiving her was God's will, so I did it by faith. Some time went by. Then one day I was drawn into a conversation involving Linda. To my amazement, I found myself defending her, saying nice things about her, feeling annoyed at the others who were being unkind toward her. It was a revelation to me. I'll never forget the kind of new joy that swept over me. For God had answered my prayer. At first I had been so angry I had said, 'Lord, You don't expect me to forgive her for what she's done.' But later, I realized it was just what I needed to do. Now I had the assurance that I had forgiven *and* forgotten. What a feeling!"

God Does Mean It

What you or I may think about a certain subject does not change the facts. So, when you find yourself bound into a kind of "You can't mean it, God" knot, you may

15

have to take "what you think" out, dust it off and evaluate it. A fair question to ask would be this: "Is my 'belief' in this instance just a means of justifying and rationalizing my behavior?" Or, "Is it that I'm actually unwilling to forgive, and I'm asking God to place His divine stamp of approval on my conduct? And that without regard to what His word plainly teaches?"

But God does "mean it." There is no honest, Christian way around it. It is God's expressed will that we should have a forgiving spirit. There is no exception. And there is no point at which He will not enable us to forgive. "Ask, and you shall receive," He has promised. You might pray something like this:

> Lord, You know how I've been hurt. You know how impossible it seems that I could ever be able to forgive the one who is responsible. Thank You for Your Spirit in me. He can and will effect the forgiveness—for I want to be forgiving, Lord— Amen.

Word it how you will. God is not looking or listening for excellent prose when we come to Him in prayer. He is interested in our sincerity, our honesty, in our being *real*. When we're asking Him for grace to be a forgiving Christian, we are zeroing into the very heart of the prayer our Lord Himself taught us to pray, "Forgive us our sins, just as we have forgiven those who have sinned against us" (Matthew 6:12, TLB).

Yes. God means it.

16

2
What If They Won't Listen?

There's a special reward for the one who initiates the reconciliation.

NORMA AND SUE had been talking over a situation that was distressing Sue. They prayed together about it, then Norma suggested, "If I were you, I think I would do whatever I could to seek forgiveness."

Sue blinked then replied, "You mean just go ask outright?" Her eyes grew wide with fright. "But what if she won't *listen?*"

Sue blinked then replied, "You mean just go ask outright?" Her eyes grew wide with fright. "But what if she won't *listen?*"

It's a valid question. What if the other person will not listen to a plea for forgiveness humbly and earnestly sought?

We certainly take a calculated risk when we go to someone we feel we have hurt in some way and ask for forgiveness. We can take comfort, however, in knowing that there's a 50/50 chance we will be met halfway. Better than that, Jesus said, "If you love Me, obey Me; and I will

17

ask the Father and He will give you another Comforter, and He will never leave you" (John 14:16, TLB).

Alma had led her teenage paper carrier, Pete, to Christ. She was overjoyed when some time later he came and told her that he felt God's call to full-time Christian service. Mrs. Green, Pete's mother, was not overjoyed. She was furious and vowed to get even with "that woman who snared my son into being religious. Who does she think she is, to come along and upset all our plans for our Peter?" Time went on and the mother grew more angry, more vindictive. She was a huge woman who had been known to throw more than one person out of her home when they displeased her. Nevertheless, Alma felt a sense of responsibility for whatever upheaval she may have caused. She determined to go and see the mother, not to apologize for leading her son to Christ, but to try to pour oil on the troubled waters in the home. It took courage as well as much prayer when Alma ventured on her mission. She was met at the door by this hostile woman's sarcastic, "Well, what do *you* want? Haven't you done enough damage?"

Their eyes met, and Alma shot up a quick prayer for grace and for the right words. Then, as the door was hesitantly opened, she stepped in. After a few moments when Mrs. Green had just sat, saying nothing, Alma eased in with, "What I've come for today is to see if you would let me explain..."

"Explain? What's to *explain?*" the mother cut in.

"Well, I thought if I could tell you how much I think of your Peter, how well and how cheerfully he's served me, that would help you to understand. I really just shared with him something that's all-important to me. Believe me, I was not trying to persuade him against your plans for him. I would never want to do that, Mrs. Green."

More silence. And Alma was still standing.

"Sit down," was not exactly a gracious invitation, but Alma felt encouraged as she accepted it.

In the ensuing ten minutes or so, the mother aired her side and some of the feelings she had about the change in her son. She even offered Alma some coffee and as they drank it, admitted, still somewhat grudgingly, "I have to say that it *hasn't hurt* Peter, what you've been telling him. He's still a good son—maybe even *better.*"

"Thank You, Lord. Thank You," Alma breathed as she left.

The outcome will not always be so satisfactory to the one who takes the first step. But, whether it is or not, there will be the inner reward that comes from doing what the Lord teaches us to do: "So if you are standing before the altar in the Temple, offering a sacrifice to God, and suddenly remember that a friend has something against you, leave our sacrifice there beside the altar and go and apologize and be reconciled to him, and then come and offer your sacrifice to God" (Matthew 5:23,24, TLB). God knows all things. He knows the response with which we will be met. Even so, He did not put restrictive clauses— "If you think they will not listen" or any other "if" in His directive to us to take the initiative.

Alma acted on what the Lord Jesus commanded. Sue, in the turmoil of mind caused by an unforgiving spirit, had forgotten that once she heeded the command and acted on it, healing could start.

It Takes Two to Tangle

When a relationship sours, we usually blame one person and consider the other a mere victim. It's not so, generally. Though it does take two to start a quarrel, it often takes just one to initiate a reconciliation. The Holy Spirit, who delights in reconciliations, generally works in both hearts when one is willing to eat humble pie and be the first to say, "I'm sorry. Will you forgive me?"

But what if "the party of the second part" is stony cold, uncooperative, will not accept the offered apology and plea for forgiveness? The root of bitterness has become deep and entwined and there is no desire for a renewed good relationship. What then? Our part is to obey, to make every effort to reach out in love and forgiveness. The results we must leave with God. We cannot do the Holy Spirit's work.

Obedience has built within it its own reward. You will

19

definitely feel better after having taken the scriptural first step. And how you *feel* will determine your body's response to the release of inner tension. As far as God is concerned you have shown a spirit of forgiveness, even though it was not met with acceptance and may indeed have brought a hostile response.

Two minister's wives, Emily and Joanne, had been quite friendly. Then one day Emily overheard Joanne say to another woman, "I like Emily, but I just wish she wasn't so *touchy.*"

Emily, rather than going to Joanne and dealing with the situation, let herself get mad at Joanne. Suddenly she was refusing any invitation Joanne gave her for a friendly cup of coffee as they had formerly often enjoyed. Nor would she explain what had caused this reversal in their relationship. Time went by. The husbands were called to new areas, and the women's paths didn't cross again. But there were many times when Joanne was saddened at the loss of a friend she had valued, even though she was aware of her touchiness (and unfortunately had said so). At last Joanne decided to do something about the relationship for her own peace of mind. She was learning that we grieve the Holy Spirit within us and forfeit peace with God when we deliberately withhold forgiveness or fail to seek forgiveness. She wrote a brief letter saying, "It has troubled me that we somehow got away from each other. If it was something I did, will you please forgive me and let's be friends again." The response? An indignant letter landed in Joanne's mailbox. "What do you mean, asking me to forgive you?" was the gist of it, and Emily spilled out the incident (now blown to great proportions in her own mind) that had caused her to terminate the friendship. Now, even though time might cause Emily to soften, there isn't anything she can do about it. For in the meantime Joanne has died — but not leaving forgiveness unsought. "Let not the sun go down on your wrath" is solid, wise caution, and because of the uncertainty of life, we might link this with another Bible verse, "Be wise: make the most of every opportunity you have for doing good" (Ephesians 5:16, TLB).

A noted psychiatrist, although himself not a Christian, is reputed to have said, "If I were a preacher, I would preach repentance and forgiveness, for nothing I know of brings such release and deep, lasting peace." And with peace comes joy. Fred, a member of our church, learned this happy truth. He was a fine, dependable man but not notably happy. He seemed always to be carrying a burden that he didn't share. One Sunday evening we heard a sermon on forgiveness. At the close of the service Fred, obviously moved, said to my husband, "Pastor, God spoke to me tonight. Now I have to do something about it. I have a brother I have not seen or spoken to since we quarreled four years ago. If I take a day off work will you go with me to see him? It's about 200 miles—but I *have* to go."

Arrangements were made, and that week the two men drove the 200 miles to see the estranged brother, Jim. They prayed earnestly for their mission but had no way of knowing how they would be received or what the outcome of their visit would be.

It was a strained reunion. The older brother was in no mood for an immediate reconciliation. But the loving concern of the younger broke some of the ice. Though Jim was too proud to admit it at the time, he was impressed that Fred had cared enough to lose a day's work and drive so far in an effort to repair a broken relationship. It wasn't until some months later, after more prayer and effort, that the two knew the joy of forgiving and being forgiven, of really being brothers again.

To Fred, it was more than worth all his time and effort. With the long-lasting burden removed, the joy in his heart spilled over wherever he went. It was as if the sun had been turned on in his life after years of dismal clouds.

Whose Responsibility Is It?

How far must we go if the other person will not come at least part way? Does he not have some responsibility to seek reconciliation?

The answer, obviously, is yes. The one who "has somewhat against thee," or who has wronged you, does have a responsibility before God to do something about it. But we must leave the other person to God; let Him work in the person's life. And, for all we know, the Lord may be speaking to the individual. But, because he cannot predict your reaction were he to take a step toward reconciliation, he is hesitant and fearful. So, if God is speaking to you, it's up to *you* to make the move. And let me say again, *you will not go alone.* This is business that the Holy Spirit delights in. He will direct your path and if you are trusting in Him, He will speak His words of reconciliation through you.

"But why should I be the one to forgive?" asked Diane, after she talked about how she and her brother had quarreled.

"Wouldn't it be more profitable, Diane, to ask, 'Why should I not be the one to ask forgiveness?'" her Sunday school teacher counseled.

The answer should be clear to anyone who has taken seriously The Lord's Prayer.

The Other Side of Forgiveness

In a book that was popular a few years ago, *Love Story* by Erich Segal, a recurring theme is, "Love means never having to say you're sorry." This may have a pretty sound, but it is on a collision course with the Scriptures. Forgiveness is predicated on repentance, saying "I'm sorry."

As a young mother, I was trying to teach this to my three-year-old Bruce. it was a Sunday afternoon, and in the home of one of our church families I had to reprimand him (he was acting like a three-year-old). Dutifully he responded with, "I'm sorry, Mommy." At which point I stood him firmly at my knee and said, "Bruce, 'being sorry' means you repent. And repentance is a turning from your sins with a determination to forsake your sins and pursue them no longer."

"Yes, Mommy," said my subdued little boy.

I never did live down that preachment as it was passed, kindly but with a degree of wonder, from one to another in our church. Nevertheless, what I pronounced was true, even if in my zeal it was inappropriately presented.

I hear some parents say, "My child does things he shouldn't; lies to me, etc. Then he says, 'I'm sorry' and figures that makes it all right for him to go ahead and lie some more, or otherwise misbehave. His 'I'm sorry' has no repentance in it." So it's good to instruct our children along these lines.

I Don't Have That Kind of Faith

"It might be OK for you," Peggy argued, "but I can't see myself going to someone and asking him to forgive me. What if he wouldn't listen? I couldn't risk that. I would have to know for sure that I would be received in the right spirit or I couldn't handle it."

Certainly it would be comforting if we could always be sure of a good outcome. And it does take faith to proceed in an unpredictable situation. But in the matter of faith we all need more than we possess. A good, ongoing prayer is, *"Lord, increase our faith"* (Luke 17:5). No one ever reaches Ph.D. status in faith.

The Lord Jesus holds out a great promise of power even if our faith is as small as a mustard seed, one of the tiniest of seeds. But, unlike a grain of sand, this grain of seed has *life* in it and the potential for growth. So even our small faith is sufficient for us to dare going to another person in a spirit of forgiveness. Our mustard seed faith as we obey God's teaching is sufficient to move a mountain of accumulated bitterness and resentment. We must take that step of faith, however small, and trust that God will move that mountain. Faith grows through being exercised. We do not strengthen our faith by standing on the sidelines watching other people prove theirs. We act on the little faith we have. God then works in the circumstances and graciously allows us to see some results. This, in turn, causes our faith to increase and also produces increasing joy. It does take faith to risk being rejected when we seek forgiveness, but the resultant joy is worth it!

A prison convert, as he read the Scriptures, felt the Lord speaking to him. He acted. He wrote his mother asking her to forgive him for all the heartache and trouble he had brought on her and on all the family. "This is something I thought I could *never* do — risk asking forgiveness," he told the chaplain, "but *Jesus is changing my life.* I don't really know if my mother and others of my family will be willing to forgive me. But I do know that the Lord Jesus knows what was in my heart when I wrote that letter to my mother."

Forgiveness by Mail?

Marie and her cousin had had a bad misunderstanding, then Marie moved to another state. "I'm going to write Cousin Jane and see if we can't patch up our friendship," she said to her husband. "Watch it," he cautioned, "better wait until you can talk face-to-face."

Good advice? Possibly. Yet, by the very nature of our mobile society — families and friends frequently moving to distant places — we often have to depend on letters and telephone calls to convey our thoughts and feelings.

In the matter of asking and receiving forgiveness we would be wise to heed certain caution lights. Let's say that you're feeling convicted about something that happened between you and a friend who has moved away. You can't go in person so, in an effort to follow Bible principles, you do the next best thing. You sit down and spell out the problem as you see it, taking your share of whatever "blame," and saying, "I'm sorry. Will you please forgive me?"

Now *you* know how you feel as you seal the letter then slip it into the mailbox on the corner. It's a good feeling. You've done your part. But what you can't know is how your letter will be received. It may well depend on how the recipient happens to be feeling, what is going on in her heart the day and hour your letter arrives. Rarely can your words convey precisely what you mean, especially in the matter of the emotions. What is missing when you are not there in person is the inflection in your voice, the eye contact that speaks what words alone can never quite say. We read with our ears as well as with our eyes. This can create a problem if the person "hears" a note you didn't intend to be a part of your letter. You need to be aware that the outcome of a written plea for forgiveness can be quite unpredictable. Forgiveness by mail? Consider all the ramifications and the other options open to you, then take the action which is most logical and will best communicate your heart attitude.

A beautiful example of a positive outcome by mail is Paul's letter by proxy, appealing for forgiveness for the runaway slave, Onesimus. Study it. It's a masterpiece of diplomacy. Paul knew the man Philemon, to whom he wrote, and he knew what his reactions would be.

I know what it is to receive a letter asking for forgiveness. It had come as a wonderful answer to prayer when I had lost track of the person's whereabouts. The letter resulted in restored friendship and a relationship filled with a deeper love than we had for each other before. Subsequently, when again we met, we just couldn't see enough of each other; the time was too short for the new sweet fellowship we had developed. (My heart glows even now as I recall the day that letter arrived and how it made me feel.) Why wait till we get to heaven to experience this joy of forgiving and being forgiven?

What If They Won't Listen?

As the young man in prison realized, God knows our hearts when we set out — *by whatever means* to seek forgiveness. We can rest our case in His hands.

You may also find that your bid for forgiveness is met with the argument, "Why should I forgive you? Don't you know how awful you made me feel?"

This is one of the times when you are master of the unspoken word. Nothing is gained by entering into the argument, which, all too often is just intended to bait you. The other person may have an I'll-have-my-pound-of-flesh-before-we-arrive-at-forgiveness attitude. It's good at such a time to ask the Lord for grace, then say quietly and without emotion in your voice, "I really am sorry and I'm asking you to forgive me." If a harangue is the response, it's best to walk away. There is no way we can persuade the person who doesn't want to be persuaded of our sincerity. Nevertheless, we can have the peace that comes from having done, in the right spirit, what God requires of us.

3

I Can't Forgive You, God

If nothing is too hard for You, God,
why don't You answer my prayer?

SARAH CAN'T FORGIVE God because her child was born with a physical handicap.

Frank declares, "I'll *never* forgive God for taking my lovely daughter."

Allan complains, "God could have prevented me from having that terrible accident that left me crippled. I can never forgive Him."

Carol blames God for the breakup of her marriage. "You could have brought Philip back to me. Why didn't You? I can't forgive You, God."

I've heard many such declamations against God.

So there is the inevitable "*Why*, God?"

Inherent in this questioning is, "I could take it if I just understood why it has to be." Furthermore, the person is inferring, "Why does this have to happen to *me*?"

We all question in this manner. I know I have, and I don't know of one person who has talked over a severe problem with me who has not intimated that the why of it perplexed him.

Most of all, we question God. This is the eternal why: why does God let it happen?

God does not have to answer. He is not obligated to explain to His creatures. This is clearly taught in Romans, "On the contrary, who are you, O man, who answers back to God? The thing molded will not say to the molder, 'Why did you make me like this,' will it?" (Romans 9:20). (Also see Isaiah 45:9.)

Nevertheless, human nature being what it is, there will always be those who are unthankful, non-accepting of their lot in life—and busy blaming God.

"But," someone new to Christian circles might question, "would a real Christian ever malign God in these ways you have described?"

The answer is yes. There are true believers in the Lord Jesus Christ whose emotions get the best of them at times. Jeri, a friend of mine, would be the first to admit that. During the time she watched her husband die a lingering, painful death from cancer, a day came when she flouted God's promises. "I tore up the Bible verses I had typed and memorized for my comfort," she told me. "And I cried, 'I don't believe You, God. I don't believe You care—or that You keep Your word.'" Within the hour the Lord sent the very help she needed. But in her ingrained bitterness against Him at that time, she spouted, "These people would have come anyway, God." (Since that time, the Lord has greatly used this woman, Jeri Krumroy, to comfort other "cancer widows.")

Closer to home, I recall all too vividly a time when I was distraught over the circumstances in which I found myself. There was not a thing I could do by myself to better things. I prayed long and fervently, reminding the Lord of His many promises to hear and answer when I call on Him. Especially I drew upon the verse in Genesis 18:14, "Is any thing too hard for God," and the resounding assertion of Jeremiah (32:17), "There is nothing too hard for Thee."

In my fruitless arguing with the Almighty, I reasoned, *If nothing is too hard for You, God, why do You not answer my heartfelt prayers? Why are You not coming to my aid, am I not Your child? And, Lord, if this that I'm asking is too hard for You, how can I put any faith in all the other promises in the Bible?*

I marvel yet at the long-suffering grace of our loving Father. Here I was practically daring Him to arrange *what I thought* was the best outcome. No thought for others concerned and what *my* solution might cost Him. No trusting God to know best. Just "make everything come out OK for me, God."

Since then I've learned — rather, I am learning — that God loves us too much to jump like an errand boy to do our bidding. He loves us too much to answer our often petulant and immature prayers. He knows the last chapter in the book of our lives, and He cares enough to take us through the circumstances that can move us into the center of His will. Sometimes it's mountains; sometimes it's valleys.

I'm finding more and more as I grow older that it pays to let God *be* God, and not to question His purposes, His ways, or His love for us. For, "He knows the way I take; when He has tried me, I shall come forth as gold" (Job 23:10).

The "Why *me*, God" is another whole area of questioning.

Why, when so many non-Christians appear to be sailing along on smooth seas should some of God's people be called on to face storms and winds of adversity?

Frequently we're riding the waves fairly well until "help" comes. For all too often family and friends come along with their well-meant support. But rather than building up the hurting individual, they come with their suggestions of who should be blamed. As if healing could come simply by pinpointing "who did it to you."

Nancy had to contend with such help. Called to the school principal's office, she was dismayed to hear, "I'm sorry, Miss Anderson, but we're having to phase out your job. The budget, you know," he said with an apologetic shrug. Nancy was understandably hurt and angered when, later, she heard that she had been the victim of politicking, and of conniving by a colleague. However she was also realistic, knowing that the administration had the last word in such matters. So she was handling the situation quite well until along came some loyal but not too wise friends saying, "It's not fair; you don't deserve such treatment; how could they do this to you, Nancy?"

By the time she had listened to these Job's comforters, her innate common sense was forsaking her. She began to be influenced by the others' thinking and ended up angry at God and complaining, "Why *me*?"

Such an approach is rarely either thoughtful or helpful. The "comforter," though well-meaning, may just not know what to say to fit the occasion and hasn't learned that a genuine, "I know you must be hurting, and I'm praying for you," can be of great comfort.

Sometimes a spiritual principle pointed out by a caring friend can be of great help. I recall a time in my own life when I was hurting, when it seemed the bottom was falling out of everything. I was far from trusting the Lord to work out His perfect will for me in the circumstance; I was grieving and griping and depressed. A minister friend listened patiently; then, very thoughtfully, offered me a piece of counsel which I have never forgotten. It was this: "Jeanette, remember that regardless of everything and everybody else, *God wants to bless you.* And He will—if you will let Him."

It must have been something God wanted me to know; and I'll always be thankful to this friend who was wise enough to realize that was all he needed to say at the time.

Regardless of the times you may have whined and complained and said (or thought, if you hadn't dared to say it), "I can't forgive You, God," He is patient and loving. If you let Him, He will bring you to a more rational position. You will see the folly, as I have, of "not forgiving God."

People can find all kinds of reasons for being angry at God. Not long ago I was a dinner guest in a Christian home where the grown-up daughter said, "My father was a saint; he really was. No matter what anyone did to him he was always quick to forgive. I would say to him, 'Dad, how can you be like you are, how can you just keep on forgiving everybody for everything. Think what people *do* to you!' But he would just smile his gentle smile and keep on forgiving. That made me mad at him. Then I became angry at God for not striking down the ones who hurt my wonderful father."

This woman's father had been dead for many years, still she harbored and kept nourishing her feelings of anger against God. In a sense she is like Jonah, who showed such anger when God did not destroy Nineveh. Prophet though he was, Jonah would have gloried in God's destruction of the inhabitants of Nineveh (else why was he so dejected at their being spared from the wrath of God?).

How important it is that we look deep inside our own hearts and search out why we "can't forgive God."

Acceptance As a Means of Coping

"I *just can't take it.*" How often we use this as an explanation of our reaction to what life brings.

Built into the inability to "forgive God" is our unwillingness to *accept* what He permits to come into our lives. We can dwell, unduly, on the "why"; this is in itself a form of unwillingness to "take it." Such rebellion can create feelings of guilt that only compound the problem.

By contrast, we will never be able to understand or explain the wonderful alchemy that produces sweetness out of sorrow, beauty from ashes, peace in the midst of pain. But who will dispute that this is so. God is the Master Designer. He knows how best to perfect that which He has created.

Just recently I saw this principle in action. A man knocked at my office door, and as I saw who he was I was at a loss for the right thing to say. His lovely wife had died two weeks earlier, in her mid-30's. They were one of God's beautiful couples, with everything to live for and a tremendous involvement with people, witnessing for Christ. I was deeply moved for I had loved this woman very much. The man broke down and cried. Then in the midst of his grief he said, with his right hand upraised, "Praise the Lord!"

This was no what-else-can-I-do gesture of resignation. Rather, it was an acknowledgment that God was at the heart of the dire circumstance, and built into his "Praise the Lord" was the affirmation that God would see him through.

With such commitment of our way unto God comes the ability to take what He sends, to see His way as the best way for us. Such acceptance can drain away any resentment or rebellion against our circumstances.

The Value of a Good Model

One person can help another find peace in the midst of severe trial. How? Through the person's non-questioning, non-rebellious attitude.

One of my dearest friends, Gwen, taught me that. Her husband, a minister, was stricken with a severe and long illness. His work for the Lord ground to a halt; the house had to be kept hushed; no visitors, few telephone calls permitted — and months of waiting while the prognosis was grim.

During these long months (knowing what my own reactions would likely have been) my friend was a walking question mark to me, and to many others. She remained calm and trusting. Later, when the Lord had graciously restored her husband to health and he was again active in his church, we talked about the difficult days.

"*What kept you going,* Gwen?" I asked.

Very thoughtfully she answered, "It was George himself (her husband). I saw how day after day he was taking it — never once did I hear him say, 'Why would the Lord let this happen?' or 'Why *Me*?' No, through it all he never questioned the Lord's will. And because he was able to take it all, the constant pain and — worse for him — the inactivity and the uncertainty of any cure, I was able to keep going and to trust the Lord. And, again and again, I would hear God saying to me, 'Be still and know that I am God.'"

My friend could endure it because her husband perceived the trial as from God, and continued to trust Him.

32

This was a new concept to me, a new insight: that one Christian's ability to take what God sends can be predicated upon the reaction of another Christian in the midst of trials. This new knowledge also put a burden upon me to be sensitive, to realize that we are all *somebody's* model.

Strength in the Stillness

"Be still"—sometimes this is the only thing God is asking of us at the time, that we keep a calm frame of mind. This in itself contributes greatly to our ability to endure. To be sure, it's a bit of a problem for some of us to "keep still," but God does not issue a mandate without giving us the inner resources for obeying, for being still—we restless, fretful creatures.

"And know that I am God." Here is where the strength ultimately lies, in the knowledge that God *is,* and that *He is for us.*

So we can be enabled to be calm and to take what God wills.

It won't always make sense to us.

Early in my own Christian life I was perplexed by the paradox of Christian suffering as it was explained to me by more mature Christians. Speaking of a certain family in our church, they said, "God must be able to trust them very much, for He's sent so much sorrow their way." The way they said it made it sound as though this were some kind of reward the Lord was handing out to the family—like a tribute for faithful service. I couldn't comprehend that. It was as if my finite mind were rejecting and tossing out such thinking as "wrong information which it could not handle." I had yet to learn the truth, the practical out-working in my own life of not me, but *Christ in me.* In my ignorance of the Bible I had never learned that God's thoughts are not my thoughts, nor my ways His ways (Isaiah 55:9). But I was to live and learn that God knows best what to use as building blocks for character and spiritual maturity and that we just rob ourselves with our childish questioning. Why me? Why don't You shove this trial off on somebody else? I can do without such an "honor."

God Knows Our Stress Tolerance

Stress—tension—anxiety levels: these related areas have captured the attention of professionals and lay people alike.

As an editor, in search of information on a subject that interested me because of articles submitted to me, I attended a seminar on Stress Management. In one session, the techniques of Biofeedback were demonstrated (on me by my volunteering). Fascinated, I watched the needle register my stress level. As it did, it came to me that God knows as no electronic device ever can tell, just what is our stress level; how much we can tolerate, and He has His ways of reducing the causes of stress which make for *dis*-stress. Accordingly He entrusts us with ever heavier burdens; but never beyond our capacity to bear them.

Why Acceptance Brings Positive Results

In accepting God's will, rather than reacting with anger, we are telling Him, "Lord, I know *You are Sovereign.* Even though I can't understand, and I certainly would never have sought this circumstance, I know that You know all about it and I can trust You."

This magic of accepting is more than a spiritual concept. Many authorities in the field of psychiatry and psychology are concluding that acceptance generates peace. Acceptance has both emotional and physical ramifications in addition to the better recognized spiritual benefits. Why is this so? Because it takes emotional energy to fight an inward battle; the tension can create physical ills, and the inner sense that we are sinning against God in our rebellion at our circumstances breeds spiritual problems. The same measure of acceptance would leave us in a far better state to be able to cope with the situation.

"It was a revelation to me," Frances said, "when I came to see that I could hold God responsible for what happens to me."

34

"How do you mean that?" I asked her (I could see certain theological problems in her statement).

"Well," she explained, "I used to fight everything that was hard for me to bear. I got plain angry at God. After all, some of the things that were happening to me shouldn't happen to a child of God! Or such was my thinking. Then, with the help of other people and by reading the Bible for myself, I began to see that God has His reasons for letting certain things happen in our lives. I guess I was growing up," she smiled with the admission. "It became just common sense, then, for me to thank God, to accept even what I couldn't understand, and place the responsibility for the outcome in God's hands."

Frances was perhaps wiser than she knew, for in giving up the fighting she was conserving rather than draining her own resources, preserving her peace of mind.

In a time of trouble or crisis nothing is more valuable than a calm attitude. The Christian, operating from a platform of God-given inner peace, should mirror this calm more than anyone else. Why then do not more of us latch on to this available potential? Paul speaks strongly to this point in Philippians 4:6, 7: "Don't worry about anything; instead, pray about everything; tell God your needs and don't forget to thank Him for His answers. If you will do this you will experience God's peace, which is far more wonderful than the human can understand" (TLB).

It is a mystery to me how this can be, but I know that it's true. One of the greatest discoveries I have ever made is that a Christian *can* have peace—real mind and soul-calming peace—*even while we still have the problem that should shatter our peace*, and us. The open secret? Acceptance: the very antithesis of not forgiving God.

"I'll do something if I know *why* I'm doing it," Kathy told me. "So why should I blindly accept anything and everything that comes my way?"

God is not disturbed or turned off by a questioning mind. It's easier for some temperaments than for others to obey without question. Nevertheless, God knows what is best for us. It's no idle whim of His that exhorts us to give thanks *in* everything and *for* everything (1 Thessalonians 5:18, Ephesians 5:20). We can skip lightly over these words. Or, as we practice what they teach, we can do much to keep ourselves emotionally stable.

Giving of thanks and acceptance cannot be separated from each other. "Thank You, God," has in it the seeds of both faith and hope: faith that God is working out His plan in our life; hope for the good outcome because He can be trusted to do what is best for us.

Lest it appear that accepting what God permits to come into our lives is a do-it-yourself effort in which we can pride ourselves, we need to hear again the words of our Lord in John 15:5, "...apart from Me you can do nothing."

Job Had the Answer

If ever anyone on earth had possible justification for being angry and saying, "I can't forgive you, God," it must have been Job. Yet he knew the secret of accepting his incredibly dreadful circumstances. When his wife (who must have been suffering also or she would be less than human), said to Job, "Curse God, and die," his reply was, "Shall we indeed accept good from God, and not adversity?" (Job 2:10, NASB). How different from the reaction of so many sufferers. Few of us reason so wisely.

Job's ultimate statement of acceptance of God's will was "Though He slay me, yet will I trust in Him" (13:15 KJV). And Job could not, as we can, read the last chapter! He could not skip from his early evil days to chapter 42 with its happy ending. The Lord restored the fortunes of Job... and "the Lord blessed the latter end of Job more than his beginning."

It takes faith to look beyond the present suffering, to keep on trusting God. But we know that, like Job, our latter days are in God's hands, and we can look forward to "dwelling in the house of the Lord forever." In the light of all the good we receive at His hand, why should we ever become angry and even think, *I can't forgive You, God?*

4
Measure for Measure

*We balance God's scales in our favor when
we are generous in forgiving others.*

JANICE STARED AT Anne, not quite believing what she
was hearing. A week earlier she had planned to have lunch
at a nearby restaurant with this new neighbor. Somehow, a
rash of things to do at home that morning had pushed the
lunch engagement out of her mind. When she thought of it
she hurried over to explain and apologize. There was no
way she could have possibly prepared herself for the volley
of indignation Anne fired at her, concluding with a
sarcastic, "And I suppose that next thing you'll be asking
me to forgive you, Janice. Well, you can just forget that."

Can it be that Anne for some reason has never prayed
the Lord's Prayer? Never uttered, "Forgive us our debts as
we forgive our debtors" (Matthew 6:12, KJV)?

There are some things that even God in Heaven cannot
do. God cannot accept a person's efforts to deliberately
withhold forgiveness from another. It is not that He has to
ration forgiveness because He might run out of it. No. It is
simply that *God has laws* and He cannot violate them. The
essence of one of His laws is, "Forgive and be forgiven."

This great scriptural principle came to me with a new

force a few years ago. My Bible reading for the day was in Matthew chapter 6, including The Lord's Prayer. It was the verses which followed that grabbed me. I read, then reread them (vv. 14, 15):

> For if you forgive men for their transgressions, your heavenly Father will also forgive you. But if you do not forgive men, then your Father will not forgive your transgressions.

The Lord Jesus obviously felt it was essential that He underscore the matter of forgiveness; what results when we do and when we do not forgive.

Forgiveness: one of the greatest themes of the Bible.

Forgiveness: in many non-Christian cultures there is no word for forgiveness — because forgiveness is unknown.

How significant, then, that in the timeless Sermon on the Mount the Master Teacher lays such emphasis on the all-importance of a forgiving spirit. "If you forgive — if you don't."

Is this dogmatic emphasis to be construed as arbitrary, God saying to us, "You play by my forgiveness rules or else"? Never! Rather, our heavenly Father (it was *Jesus* who taught us to call God by this tenderest of names) is doing us the greatest of all favors in teaching and requiring us to be forgiving.

As You Forgive

What does the Bible mean by "as" in the context of forgiving?

Let's look at another "as": "As [a man] thinketh in his heart, so is he" (Proverbs 23:7, KJV).

Clearly we are dealing with the laws of cause and effect. We do something or don't do it — and something happens. Even a very young child can quickly grasp that.

"As" can refer to the manner in which we forgive, how we express it. Some people say, "I forgive you," and their tone and gracious attitude give reality to the three often carelessly spoken words. They leave the forgiven person *feeling* forgiven.

By contrast, I've heard a child say — and I wonder where

this insight comes from—"She says she forgives me, but she really hasn't. I can tell." Sometimes the child has sensed a "You don't deserve to have me forgive you," in the other's so-called forgiveness. It's a condescending put-down rather than genuine forgiveness.

Akin to the latter is the conditional, "I'll forgive you if you don't do it again." "The way my aunt says it," a teenager admitted, "just makes me want to do it again. She doesn't trust me to have learned a lesson when I admit I was wrong and ask her to forgive me."

Then there's the holier-than-thou kind of "forgiveness": a pharisaical mouthing of the words, while the expression is really indicting the other person. There's a note of "*I* would never be guilty of such an offense. See what a righteous person I am, and how magnanimous I am in forgiving you." That is a thousand light years away from Christian forgiving of one another.

Another kind of "as" speaks of the *extent,* the measure of forgiveness, the totality of it. The Bible makes many references to the limitlessness of God's forgiveness. None is more graphic and all-encompassing than "He has removed our sins as far away from us as the east is from the west" (Psalm 103:12, TLB).

Have you ever tried to bridge the distance between the East and the West?

Have you ever succeeded in arriving at the East from the West? (I live in California—as "west" as you can be in the continental United States. Frequently I travel to New York—east all the way! But I never arrive at the east. There is always more "east" for our east and west is relative. Kipling was stating universal as well as poetic truth when he wrote, "East is East and West is West, and never the twain shall meet."*

Significantly, God does not submit, "As far as the *North* is from the *South*" as the extent of His forgiveness. That would be limited, for, having gone north to the Pole, we then go south. How precise, how explicit is the Word of God. How limitless beyond all measure is His forgiveness; and it's *ours* by faith!

*From *Ballad of East and West,* by Rudyard Kipling.

Probably the most important meaning of "*As* you forgive" is the genuineness of it. The forgiven person is aware of the other's sincerity. There is no "hidden agenda" about it, no *saying* I forgive you, then figuratively filing the offense to bring it up for review the next time something comes up.

A Form of Giving

Luke writes of *for*giving in the context of giving.

> And do not pass judgment and you will not be judged; and do not condemn, and you shall not be condemned; pardon, and you will be pardoned. Give, and it will be given to you; good measure, pressed down, shaken together, running over, they will pour into your lap. For whatever measure you deal out to others, it will be dealt to you in return (Luke 6:37, 38).

Is not forgiving a form of giving? Perhaps the highest form? If that be so, we do well to look to the size of our measuring cup.

Jean was talking about forgiveness with some friends. "I can forgive some things," she admitted, "but there are others..." Her raised eyebrows and shrug of the shoulders finished the sentence. Then as though to justify herself she added, "It's hard to forgive *everything*."

"Give me a 'for instance,'" Susan suggested in an airy tone. "I wouldn't want to be guilty of one of the things you don't forgive." This brought a little laughter until another of the friends said, "It's not really funny, you know."

Apparently Jean has her own measuring cup for dispensing forgiveness. It's big enough for some things; not for others. It's not scriptural size.

An Extra Dimension

Paul the apostle shows the great sensitivity of one who has, himself, been forgiven much. "Forgive *and comfort*," (2 Corinthians 2:7) he advocates. A step beyond forgiving, going the other mile. Paul's knowledge of human nature tells him that the forgiven person may still harbor strong feelings that may overwhelm him. So Paul urges "Reaffirm your love for him" (v. 8). The apostle is, in effect, making a bid for emotional support following the forgiveness, rather than a mere verbal gratuity.

My daughter Jeannie, a missionary in Bangladesh, mentioned in a letter that a Christian national had been drawn into a group who had been stealing from the missionaries. This man confessed and repented. But, though the missionaries freely forgave him and treated him kindly, he was abject in his feelings of guilt. Jeannie wrote, "I'm going to devote this next week to 'restoring such a one'" (Galatians 6:1, KJV).

Today's psychologists make much of the term *affirming people,* and they mean the same as Paul meant: reassure, reinforce the person. "Validate" is another modern term for the same offering of comfort. We can do our human best in this area. But only the Spirit of God, whispering assurance that our repentance and plea for forgiveness have been heard, can make us, the forgiven ones, *feel* forgiven and loved.

Rooting Out the Weeds

"But I *have* forgiven him," John insisted. "I've told him so. What more am I expected to do? The Bible says we should forgive one another and that's what I've done."

No doubt John was being quite truthful. He had *intellectually* forgiven whoever it was who had offended him. He had followed the letter of the law. But that's not enough. Yet some people experience difficulty in forgiving on the emotional level. They may want to forgive and hold no grudges, but find that some of the bitterness returns. John's "What more am I expected to do?" savors of such a personality.

The Bible says we must forgive and the law of our emotions tells us we should forgive; for resentment and bitterness are destructive to mental and physical health (to say nothing of the spiritual ramifications). So, should it not be easy to forgive?

But is it?

Sally was working in her garden one day when an older

41

woman came by and, just to make conversation, asked, "What are you doing?"

"Trying to find some flowers under all these weeds. I guess I let things get a bit out of hand."

The human heart can be likened to a garden. It often becomes entangled with the weeds of bitterness and resentment and periodically needs weeding.

Forgiveness is a great beautifier. It clears away the ugly debris from the garden of our life and then we can see the flowers.

But how to do this rooting out?

A psychologist with years of successful practice, Dr. Jeannette Acrea, offers these proven steps:

First, we need to approach the matter positively. God *says* to forgive, and He will never give a command that is impossible for us to carry out. "For this is the love of God, that we keep His commandments; and His commandments are not burdensome" (1 John 5:3). As we trust God and His character we have this assurance.

Second, we have to dig deep and find the weeds of resentment, hostility, and whatever other "little foxes are spoiling the vines." If we do not acknowledge their presence and do something to get rid of them, they will take over the whole garden. (The reverse is likewise true. Californian horticulturists have developed a plant that can tolerate smog. Known as "Freeway Daisies," the flowers come in lovely shades of pink, purple, and white. In short order this plant takes over a hillside or freeway bank, beautifying the landscape while eradicating the weeds.)

Third, pull out the weeds. How? Jane had felt lifelong resentment against her parents. Having been helped to recognize this, she then openly acknowledged her anger and hostile feelings. She expressed them. In doing so she discovered something deeper — a deadlier weed had been allowed to flourish. She began to realize *why* she had not been able or willing to forgive her mother and dad. (She wanted *them* to hurt as she felt they had caused her to suffer through the years.) Her feeling was, *If I forgive them, they won't suffer. And why should they get off scot free?*

The deadly element was vengeance. And God's Word plainly teaches, "Never pay back evil for evil. 'Vengeance is mine, I will repay' says the Lord" (Romans 12:17, 19). Not that God is vengeful. No. But God alone is competent to judge fairly. He doesn't need us to help Him now or on Judgment Day! His repayment is without a desire to get even (which Jane exhibited), or malice.

Another destructive weed in Jane's garden was that she wanted her parents to be tied to her and she to them, through her consuming anger. So she had to be willing to surrender her unhealthy and unholy feelings — these deeply implanted weeds, and root them all out. To do this she would need emotional and intellectual insight. It meant that she must become aware of how the weeds permeated various facets of her life, hurting emotionally, often physically and certainly *spiritually* the person she could otherwise be.

Here are two indisputable reasons for having a forgiving spirit: we should always be willing to forgive the *penitent* for their sake, and we need to forgive the *im*penitent for our sake, "For whatever measure you deal out to others, it will be dealt to you in return" (Luke 6:38).

The Part Our Will Plays

Our exhibiting a will to be forgiving plays a big part in God's leading in our lives.

Fred had been in sales with a major national company for thirty-two years. In late 1978 they reorganized their New York office, where Fred worked, and he was declared redundant. He was then assigned to Stamford, Connecticut where there was no office. At the time he bitterly resented the move; he was angry over the whole change and with everyone involved in the move. In just seven months he was making a success of his new territory. But he still nursed the grudge. Fred's wife, anxious to help her husband overcome his bitterness, suggested, "Fred, it's time we got down on our knees and asked God *to help you to forgive* the man who did this to you."

After several weeks Fred agreed. They did get on their

knees. Fred did seek the Lord's help to be truly forgiving in his heart. And the Lord released him from the bonds of bitterness. Fred did forgive the other man.

I can hear someone say, "That's all right for some people, this being able to forgive. But if you only knew what I've gone through at the hands of other people. You would know it would take more forgiveness than anyone has." Or, as a friend of mine said, "Jeanette, it would take more forgiveness than *I* have for me to say to so-and-so, 'I forgive you.'" Too late I thought of how I might have responded to her honest admission. I could have reminded her that none of us has "enough forgiveness"; forgiveness isn't a human commodity. I would not have it, my friend would not have it, but for the indwelling Spirit of God in the believer.

We must remember that forgiveness is not a *feeling:* it is a *choice* we deliberately make.

First comes the determination: "I *will,* by faith." We never do anything (if we are rational) apart from willing to do it. The will must tell the brain, which then activates the hand to write a forgiveness note, the feet to go in person to seek forgiveness when we ought to. The feeling comes later, so if we wait until we "feel like it," we may wait too long.

In a sense, a forgiving spirit is an investment, perhaps the best of all investments. It brings guaranteed returns. In choosing to invest ourselves by fully forgiving someone who has sinned against us, we reap the rich rewards of being forgiven by God—and feeling it.

Why should we expect generous returns if our investment has been meager?

5
Why Don't They Change?

Some people don't change because others won't.

"I WOULD BE willing to forgive Craig," Sarah said, "but it does no good. He doesn't change. It's been this same way for eight years. He drinks, then comes home and disrupts everything. The next day he says, 'I'm sorry. I *swear* I'll never do it again.' But it's just *words*. And I'm tired of being the one who does the forgiving. And besides," she continued, "isn't there another side to this forgiveness business?"

"What?" her friend Gladys asked.

"Well, by continuing to accept his insincere apologies, am I not contributing to his problem?" Then, in frustration that she did not attempt to hide, she spouted, "*Why* can't I change Craig?"

"Sarah," Gladys asked gently, "have you thought that you and I are not in the changing business? *God* is."

While it's true that we are not generally able by our own efforts to effect needed change in someone, sometimes we can help them to recognize the need for change in themselves.

Irene, a pastor's wife, learned this secret after many years of helping people with their problems. She found that it often worked when she said — *without sounding judgmental about it* — "You have a choice. You can keep on the way you are, but — have you thought of the consequences?"

In one instance the woman seeking help was a personable young woman named Susanne, a recent convert. She was having a difficult time breaking some of her former habits, even though she was an ardent witness to her new-found Lord. Her greatest problem involved relationships with men. "I know what the Bible says," she would explain, "but not how to get victory." So she slipped back into her old ways, sought God's forgiveness, slipped back, sought forgiveness — over and over.

"I've been praying especially for you," Irene told her the next time she came, "and the verse that keeps coming to me as I pray is, 'Keep back thy servant from presumptuous sins; let them not rule over me'" (Psalm 19:13).

"Let me see that verse! I didn't know anything like that was in the Bible. That's *me*! I'm letting sin dominate me," Susanne freely admitted.

Irene helped her find the verse for herself in the psalm. As she read on, "Then shall I be blameless...," a longing look spread on her face. "*Blameless*. How wonderful it would be to have such a feeling!"

The outcome was that Irene was able to help this new Christian to begin to appropriate the "escape" route God has provided in the time of temptation. Together they memorized 1 Corinthians 10:13,

> No temptation has overtaken you but such as is common to man; and God is faithful, who will not allow you to be tempted beyond what you are able, but with the temptation will provide the way of escape also, that you may be able to endure it.

By realizing she had had an "escape route" ever since her conversion, and having acknowledged her guilt, Susanne was in a position to grow in grace and in ability to yield less and less to temptation. She had everything going for her because she was willing to change.

Your Motive Is Showing

Sylvia went to her pastor and said, "Pastor, will you please pray with me that my father-in-law will change. If he would only accept the Lord!"

In the course of the interview, Sylvia confided, "I can't stand the way things are with Phil's dad living with us. It's hard for me to forgive him for spilling his cigarette ashes on the rug and — oh, a whole lot of things," she added with a wide gesture of her arms. "And our car smells of tobacco whenever we take him anywhere with us. It's *so embarrassing.*"

"So you want me to pray for Phil's dad that he'll be saved," the pastor commented.

"Yes, will you, please. It would make such a difference."

"I'll pray for your father-in-law's salvation," agreed the pastor, "but I have to be honest with you. I will not be praying for the same reason you want me to."

"What do you mean?" Sylvia asked. "Does it matter to God what the reason is? Isn't he interested in everybody coming to Christ? The Bible says that He is not willing that any should perish."

"Right. God does want everyone to be saved and He has made provision in Christ. What I'm saying is that you would do well to take a close look at your motives in wishing your father-in-law would become a Christian."

Sylvia was visibly annoyed with her pastor. She bustled out of his study muttering to herself about not being able to understand *preachers.*

Sylvia — and others with similar petitions — are, if they would stop and ponder, in the best position of anyone to answer their own prayers.

What would be likely to draw an unsaved in-law to Christ? Would not a loving concern for him *as a person,* especially if this were a new attitude he was sensing toward him, tend to soften him, dispose him to listen or at least to wonder what had caused the change? It might be hard for him to long resist if he learned that his daughter-in-law's concern was that he would miss out on the joys of heaven; that it was *his* interests she was thinking of.

On the other hand, her desiring his salvation so that the house and car would be free of tobacco smoke would indicate that Sylvia herself is the one who needs to ask forgiveness, then begin to change.

Change Comes Later

Haven't you ever heard someone say, "If only Mary would change, there might be some hope for her." It's not a malicious statement; it's not demeaning Mary. But it is certainly revealing a distorted theology if the person means, "The Lord would save her if she would only change."

How much changing did you do in order to gain salvation? How much did I change? How much change does it take to get God's attention?

The glory of the gospel is that, as we read in Revelation 1:5, "He loved us and washed us from our sins": *in that order,* loved then washed us. We do it in reverse. We see a child playing in a mud puddle, dirty all over. We shake our head and sigh, "She would be so *lovable* if she were just all cleaned up."

Well might we sing the old Ira Sankey hymn,

How helpless and hopeless
We sinners had been,
If he never had loved us
Till cleansed from our sin.

Unto Him who has loved us
And washed us from sin;
Unto Him be the glory
Forever — Amen.*

If we had to be on probation until we had changed sufficiently to merit salvation, our case *would* be hopeless.

Change *follows* conversion. It is God's intent that we should keep on changing. A changed life is normally the

*Sacred Songs & Solos #1023. Marshall, Morgan & Scott — no copyright shown.

visible sign that we have been born into Christ's kingdom. So, expecting Mary to change and ready herself for the salvation experience is putting too great a burden on her. Also, it is discrediting God's promises, which are to the contrary: "I am the way," Jesus said (John 14:6). There is no other way. "Now you are clean"—not by your own washing—but "by the word I have spoken to you" (John 15:3).

How many will miss God's heaven because some well-meaning person suggested that salvation is a do-it-yourself, clean-up campaign!

Reversing the Question

Sometimes we have to ask, Why *do* they change?

Hal and Linda accepted the Lord as young marrieds. They made great strides, were wholehearted in their involvement with their church. They were up early Sunday morning to collect boys and girls from wherever they could, driving them to Sunday school. They listened intently to older Christians. That was ten years ago.

Where are Hal and Linda today, spiritually? Far from God, if we can determine this by their attitudes and interests.

What happened? Hal's company moved him to a distant city. They immediately sought out a church affiliated with the one they had regretfully left.

"It was *unbelievable*," Hal said. "All those people were interested in was *numbers*. My wife had been sick and she was still quite weak the first Sunday we attended that church. And people pushed her, stepped on her toes—just to crowd more people in. We tried to make allowances; we knew this was not our wonderful home church where we had met Christ and found a loving family. We kept on going for a while. But nobody cared whether we did or not. Our offers to help where we could were spurned; 'We like people to be around for a while, get to know us better, then we find jobs for them,' they explained. Gradually we got discouraged—and we found plenty of people outside the church who liked us for ourselves and were happy to have

49

us around. *'Who needs church?'"* was his cynical remark, but his eyes were sad as he made it. Being hurt by other Christians is what made them change. It is true, of course, that the actions of others is no excuse for a falling away from trust in God, but such things do happen.

Contrast Eunice's case. Here is a young, adventurous woman who told me, "I had tried *everything,* gone every-where — Katmandu — India — wherever I thought I would find the answer to life's riddle. For I knew there had to be a great Somebody; my medical studies convinced me that the human body is a miracle, with its 30 trillion cells functioning as no computer ever manufactured could hope to do. I read everything people told me to read, Eastern philosophies of religion in particular. But the emptiness wouldn't go away. It was all phony."

"How did you move from the phony to the *real?*" I asked when she paused. "Some place you went? Something new you read?"

"Oh," she became very animated, "neither. It was special *people.* I suddenly met some students who were so *alive* — so joyful — so genuinely excited about life (by contrast with the blase or the fanatic ones I'd spent most of my life with) that I began to ask questions. But what impressed me in addition to their excitement about life was that they accepted me *as I was.* All the other groups I had been involved with wanted me to change — to do this or that, then I might be able to join them. Not these students. They invited me to their study groups, they let me ask all the questions I cared to ask (looking back I realize how naive, even how stupid I must have sounded much of the time, but nobody made me feel out of place or embarrassed)."

Again she paused, then her eyes lit up as she said, savoring every word, "They told me about a *Person*, not a religion. They had the secret for which I had been searching and because they showed love to me, I could believe what they were saying about Jesus."

"What about the emptiness?" I asked, smiling.

"It's gone — it's gone," she answered, "and my life is full and wonderful."

A few months ago I met and talked with a young systems

computer operator. In the course of the conversation I asked, "How did you come to know Christ as your Savior, David?"

"I was in college," he explained, "studying music — rock music — my goal being to travel with a band. Things weren't going all that well. The equipment needed to get started in that field was so costly, and my folks were certainly not overjoyed at my career choice. I was pretty down about the whole thing. But I kept running into a girl at school who was always on top. She seemed so happy and smiling. One day I just came right out and asked her, 'What makes you so happy all the time?' And she told me. Very simply she explained that she had Christ in her heart and He gave her peace no matter what was happening in her life.

"What it was she had, I knew I wanted it, so she shared with me how I could have that same joy she had. With something she called the Four Spiritual Laws, she made sin and separation from God, and how I could be reconciled to Him, simple enough that I could understand and believe that Jesus died for me, and that He was willing to accept me into His family if I would receive Him as my Savior. There was more, but that's the essence of how I became a Christian. I'll always be thankful to God for that happy girl who didn't keep her secret to herself. Now, here I am, happily a part of a Christian organization instead of bumping around trying to make a living with rock music."

If these instances would teach us anything, it is that we need, periodically, to examine our everyday attitudes and ask, "If I were the only Christian someone would ever meet, what impression of Christ and Christian living would that person have?"

We may have to get down on our knees and ask the gracious Lord to forgive us (1) for not being aware of how we can cause another to stumble through our indifference; (2) for not reflecting a true image of a joy-filled life that will draw others toward Him.

A Problem of Complexity

Katherine's ongoing problem is not uncommon but it frequently goes undiagnosed. She confided, after I had spoken at a meeting, "I heard what you were saying. I understood perfectly, but it raises a great big problem for me. My husband mistreats me, but he insists he loves me. I love him and I do try to forgive and not bring things up again. But what am I supposed to do when there's no change? Oh, he sounds *so sincere,*" she said shaking her head in confusion. "And most of the time he's a caring, warm-hearted Christian man. I just don't understand it and I'm at my wit's end as to what to do."

A paradox? Yes. And I know of others like this man. They do things that are totally reprehensible while at the same time they claim to be and much of the time act like normal Christians.

Puzzled by this Dr. Jekyll and Mr. Hyde complex, I asked a psychiatrist who is a Christian if he had any explanation of such dual behavior. Here is the essence of his discussion of the topic:

"I would be a loss to explain such behavior, if we were just one-part beings. But we are not. God has made us with bodies, and with souls, and with emotions. We're tri-part human beings and invariably, when one part 'goes wrong' one or both of the other parts are affected. The *physical* affects the *psychological* and the *spiritual.*"

"What went wrong with the man who loves the Lord and yet mistreats his wife?" I asked.

"Simple," he replied. "I would stake my reputation on it that here is a man who has a neurological impairment in the *area of judgment.* What I mean is that while he may be functioning well physically and spiritually, he has lost the sense of right and wrong. In a sense, he's functioning without a conscience. That's why he *sounds* sincere, but his behavior does not reflect that he is."

Human beings are not noted for being aware of their own weaknesses and failings. It would help, then, if we had a friend who would point out the areas in which we need to change. But most people would hesitate to risk a relationship by being completely frank. If they did, we might mistrust their motive and intent.

But the Bible is such a friend.

Likening the Word of God to a mirror in which we see our true selves, Paul writes in 2 Corinthians 3:18,

> But we all, with unveiled face beholding as in a mirror the glory of the Lord, are being transformed into the same image from glory to glory, just as from the Lord, the Spirit (2 Corinthians 3:18).

When our earnest prayer is, "Oh, to be like Thee," we will *want* to change, and welcome anything that enables us to change.

6

The Part
Confession Plays

We freely confess our little faults,
to persuade others we have no big ones.

THE TOPIC IN the couples' group Bible study was Confession.

Sandra, a new Christian, created a little merriment with her naive "I like the Bible verse that says that confession is good for the soul." Some snickered and one of the men quipped, "Yes, and I suppose you also like the verse, 'Cleanliness is next to godliness.'"

After the good-natured teasing subsided, the group leader said seriously, "Sandra's not so far wrong; even though the Bible doesn't say it in these words, confession *is* good for the soul." He smiled in Sandra's direction, then continued. "In fact, confession is a must if we would know forgiveness.

"As I see it, scripturally there are three steps: confession of sin; genuine repentance; fruits of repentance."

"You said 'scripturally'; which scripture verses do you have in mind?" asked Jean. That set the group searching with concordance for what the Bible really says on the

55

subject of confession and forgiveness. It was a long session; they finally came up with three points, and related Bible verses:

Luke 17:1-6 — "I repent" precedes the forgiveness.

Matthew 18:15 — The sinning brother is to be given a chance to repent and then be forgiven

Matthew 3:8 — There must be signs (fruits) of repentance. Likewise, Acts 26:20.

Different Things to Different People

"Confession" is, to some people, a ritual and nothing more. To others, it's an easy way of expiating their known sins or faults and going on their merry way.

This can be true even of some Christians in their confessions to God. After all, confession is simply agreeing with God about your sin. When you confess your sin to God, you are acknowledging that you recognize the sinful behavior or attitude God already sees. Confession is meant to humble us as we enumerate our sins before a holy and just God. But without a proper view of our sins and of God's righteousness, even confession can become a meaningless exercise.

Jerry had that problem. He could inflict hurt on someone else — and he often did — then rationalize, *"I said I'm sorry.* Isn't that enough for you?" His tone indicated that he was the victim rather than the offender. No confession. No repentance, or certainly no *signs* of repentance.

Some people use confession as a means of drawing attention to their superior spirituality. "I'm tired of hearing Mildred's 'confessions,'" Anne said to herself. "Seems she just wants me to know how humble and contrite she is. Why doesn't she confess to the Lord and be done with it. He is the one she needs to impress, not me."

The Washing of Dirty Linen

Another aspect of confession leaves something to be questioned.

The Bible is clear as to the value of our confessing our faults one to another (James 5:16). However, this whole area of confession and full disclosure in our society which so advocates "open communication" can cause more hurts than it heals. And, as James points out, the purpose of confession is that we then pray for one another and the result is healing (of rifts? or sensitive, injured feelings?). This doesn't seem to indicate a confession before a corporate body such as the church. Confess "one to another" is the admonition.

Many Bible teachers I have listened to have differentiated between faults and sins, emphasizing that *we confess our sins only to God*. Faults can be areas of weakness or stumbling and fumbling that we are all guilty of from time to time. But there is nothing premeditated or evil-intentioned about them. Nevertheless, they may affect another person and cause some degree of offense. When we become aware of having done some such thing, we do need to confess and make it right if possible. Sara, for example, misread an announcement of a church function then passed on the wrong date to another person. In so doing, Sara certainly was not willfully sinning. The other woman, Frances, was understandably disappointed when she and her family missed the church function. It was too late when Sara learned of her mistake. Nevertheless, to clear the air and heal any possible breach she confessed her fault in the matter. This was, as we say, no big deal and it would have made little difference who heard Sara's confession.

There is, however, a kind of confessing that goes way beyond the injunction of James (the parties involved taking care of it between themselves). We see in many church circles a "confessing one to another" that becomes in essence a corporate washing of dirty linen. This spilling of sinful behavior edifies no one, God is not honored, and many people are hurt. Young or new Christians in particular may become confused. I know how I would have felt as a new Christian, with all my unsullied ideas of what a real Christian is, to hear a seasoned church member get up and "tell all" to the entire church body. In fact, one of the beautiful things in my memory of those early days as a believer in Christ was that He seemingly guarded me from things that might have disillusioned me, until such time as I was able to take it. Not that any Christian is ideal in all his behavior or that any of us ever reaches perfection down here. Nevertheless, the non-Christian or even the new believer tends to set high, unrealistic standards for the professing Christian. It was months before I detected the behavioral flaws in my new friends, and I recall being slightly disappointed as well as surprised when my bubble was finally burst. So we need to think well before confessing sin in an open meeting.

Even older Christians can be made to stumble when they are treated to a recital of another church member's sins. Moreover, such public confession is like a prairie fire, hard to contain, traveling fast and leaving destruction in its wake.

Still another adverse consequence of open confession is that it almost always militates against the restoration of the one who has confessed. For the public has a long memory. It does need to be said, however, that there have been instances when such confession of even gross sin has melted a congregation. Their attitude has then been Galatians 6:1 all the way:

> Dear brothers, if a Christian is overcome by some sin, you who are godly should gently and humbly help him back onto the right path, remembering the next time it might be one of you who is in the wrong (TLB).

The crux would appear to be the kind of person hearing the confession: godly and aware that he too is prone to sin.

Pastor S. was accused of falling into sin involving a woman he had counseled in his church study. The deacons, after hearing his confession, his plea for forgiveness and his resignation, met to consider what steps they should take.

Said the godly chairman, "Men, it may well be that we have failed. I, for one, have not upheld the pastor as I should. He is God's servant, and he has served the Lord and this church well for the years he has been with us. And Satan is never happy over such spiritual success."

Others agreed that they also felt they had been negligent. They called the pastor into their meeting. "Please don't resign, Pastor," they urged. "God has forgiven you. Can we do less?"

It was an emotional scene as each man in turn assured the pastor of his forgiveness, "and you can count on us to pray for you more earnestly and consistently," they promised.

The congregation accepted the deacons' recommendation that their pastor be given a second chance, and that church moved into a whole new area of blessing and growth.

This church was not condoning their pastor's falling into sin. Rather, their decision was based on "If any man be overtaken in a sin": they viewed the situation as his having been tempted (overtaken by temptation) and temporarily succumbing, not as one who has committed deliberate, premeditated, and prolonged sin. They also heeded the admonition of 1 Corinthians 10:12, "Therefore let him who thinks he stands take heed lest he fall."

Forgiveness wipes out sin. It does not do away with the consequences. The love of God forgives, but the justice of God must also be met. "As we sow, so shall we reap" is both a natural and a spiritual principle. God would deal with Pastor S.; He did not need the congregation to help Him dispense chastisement. And the wise board of deacons recognized what their part was by their forgiveness.

Playing the Blame Game

Frank had cheated on an exam. Confronted by the teacher, he turned on the person whose paper he had copied. "It's Anne's fault," he insisted, "if she had kept her paper away from me I would not have copied from her, so it's *her* fault," he repeated.

"Miriam will never admit *responsibility*," Anita said in obvious frustration. "She has an excuse for everything. If I heard her say *even once,* 'It was my fault. Please forgive me,' I wouldn't believe my ears."

Blame-throwing. It's as old as the human race.

Adam started it.

We know the story recorded in Genesis chapter three

only too well. The serpent came with his insidious:

"Has God said 'You shall not eat from any tree of the garden?'"

And the woman said to the serpent, "From the fruit of the trees of the garden we may eat; but from the fruit of the tree which is in the middle of the garden, God has said, 'You shall not eat from it or touch it, lest you die.'"

And the serpent said to the woman, "You surely shall not die! For God knows that the day you eat from it, your eyes will be opened, and you will be like God, knowing good and evil" (Genesis 3:1-3).

Eve believed the devil's lie, "You surely shall not die!" She capitulated to the serpent. She opened Pandora's box, and its contents have plagued humanity ever since.

Adam seemingly didn't even question her when she gave him some of the forbidden fruit. Then came the reckoning. And what did the guilty pair do? First they tried to hide from God. Then, when He asked if they had eaten from the forbidden tree, Adam said, "The woman whom Thou gavest to be with me, she gave me from the tree, and I ate" (Genesis 3:12). In essence Adam was saying, "It's Your fault, God. If You hadn't brought this woman on the scene, I wouldn't have been tempted and disobeyed. Everything was all right until You brought *her* to me."

Eve was quick to catch on to the defense mechanism of excusing herself by tossing the blame elsewhere. Questioned by God she answered, "The serpent deceived me, and I ate" (Genesis 3:13).

I wonder, did Adam and Eve, on their sad, tragic journey out of Eden ever pause and say one to the other, "I was wrong; it was all my fault?" Or, did they argue and blame each other the rest of their exiled lives?

Whatever they did, mankind has been playing the blame game ever since. Contrast David the "confessor":

David, the "sweet singer of Israel"
David, the strong man, killer of lions and a giant
David, writer of some of the most beautiful and

reverent thoughts and words in all the Bible—
in all literature
David, the man of innumerable good qualities and
noted achievements
David—the "apple of God's eye"

Feed all this information into a computer. Then add the account of David's gross sin of adultery. The incongruous input would probably scramble the computer's system!

Yet sinner he was.

David could have excused himself before man, no doubt. After all, he was the king, and can't kings do anything they please, have anything (anyone) they want? He could also have argued, "God, You know I'm a man of action. I was bored, stuck here as a figurehead," or, "Lord, You gave us our emotions; You know how a man can be stirred by a beautiful woman." There's nothing like that in the record.

To be sure, David did not immediately confess. It took the prophet Nathan, as he aroused David's "righteous indignation" to make the king see his sin in all its heinousness (2 Samuel 12:1-9).

Faced with his sin, no one was more repentant than David. Psalm 51 is the heartcry of a man acutely conscious of his gross deed. God heard David's plea for cleansing, forgiveness, and for restoration: "Create in me a clean heart, O God, and renew a right spirit within me."

Was David comfortable while the sin remained unconfessed, unforgiven? Oh, no. In Psalm 32 he admits,

When I kept silent about my sin, my body wasted away through my groaning all day long. For day and night Thy hand was heavy upon me; my vitality was drained away as with the fever-heat of summer (vv. 3, 4).

But that same Psalm offers priceless comfort to the one who will acknowledge his sin and seek forgiveness as did David. He writes (vv. 1, 2) of the blessedness of the one whose *transgressions are forgiven*, whose *sin is covered*, and to whom the Lord does not *impute iniquity*.

Three-fold forgiveness: forgiveness of transgression— crossing the legal boundary (breaking one of God's Commandments); forgiveness of sin—of falling short of God's mark; forgiveness of iniquity—a covering up of immorality.

David had triple assurance. His sin was taken away, it was covered with the lid of God's forgetfulness and it was canceled, never to appear on his account again.

Confession does away with destructive guilt feelings; forgiveness eases the pangs of conscience.

As an editor, I did a reader survey of the emotional problems that most beset Christians. Far ahead of any other was GUILT. Yet we have the assurance, "There is therefore now no condemnation for those who are in Christ Jesus. For the law of the Spirit of life in Christ Jesus has set you free from the law of sin and of death" (Romans 8:1,2).

We do not have to live crippled by debilitating guilt feelings.

The Bible is clear as to the price David paid for his sins of adultery and of connivance to kill the husband of Bathsheba. The child Bathsheba bore to David died (2 Samuel 12:12-18). God had decreed "Thou shalt not commit adultery," and "Thou shalt not kill." There was no way that God could justly wink at a lawbreaker, even though in this case he was "the apple of God's eye" (Psalm 17:8). The sin of the father was visited upon the child, according to the law.

The love of God forgave David when he repented; the law of God demanded justice, for "Shall not the Judge of all the earth do right?" (Genesis 18:25).

Just Sorry They're Caught

Not all "confessions" can be taken at face value.

I heard a store manager say, "No one is more contrite than the shoplifter who is caught with the goods. The person will say 'I'm so sorry, I don't know why I did it,' all the while hoping *and expecting* that I'll reply, 'Oh, that's all right, I understand,' or some such exonerating assurance.

I've heard all the excuses and the pleas for forgiveness," he added.

Human behavior and the reasons behind it have not changed through the centuries. The Bible, always revelatory of man's actions and reactions, paints a vivid picture of "confession" for fear of reprisal. Joseph's brothers had diabolically mistreated him as a seventeen-year-old. Only the intervention of one of them, Reuben, saved his life. They then sold him into slavery and told their father a wild animal had killed him (Genesis, chapter 37). Years pass and, in the providence of God, Joseph has become comptroller of the very land into which he was taken as a slave, Egypt. It's a dramatic tale, and in chapter 49, Joseph's father, the Patriarch Jacob, dies. Joseph had rewarded the evil his brothers did to him with remarkable good, with never a recrimination. "But," said they to one another, "that was while Father was alive. He spared us for Father's sake. What will he do to us now?

What if Joseph should bear a grudge against us and pay us back in full for all the wrong which we did to him! (Genesis 50:15).

Their dire expectations of Joseph reveal much of their own character. They attributed to Joseph what they knew their own thinking would be in the situation. And they quaked in their sandals.

So they sent a messenger to Joseph, saying, "Your father charged before he died... Please forgive, I beg you, the transgression of your brothers and their sin, for they did you wrong" (vv. 16, 17).

It wasn't even their own confession; they used their dead father to intercede for them.

So we cannot always put much stock in verbally expressed "repentance."

"Karen is just a naughty child," a frustrated fellow-employee complained. "She does all kinds of unacceptable things, snitches from company supplies, whispers untrue things that get the rest of us into trouble, gets people to cover up for her when she's late, all kinds of things! Then when she's caught doing one of these things she has the sweetest way of saying, 'O forgive me. I'm *so* sorry.'"

It *is* a childish trait (and manipulative as well) to ask forgiveness as the alternative to just punishment. It's a mark of maturity to confess, "I did commit a sin (against man or God). Humanly speaking, I do not deserve to be forgiven, but *I am sorry* and I'm asking that you please forgive me."

When Former Sins Rankle

Jill came to know Christ as her Savior some years after she graduated from high school. "I know the Lord saved me," she said, "but when I was in high school I did some cheating—quite a bit. Now I'm often troubled about that. I would like to get in touch with my teachers and confess that sin. But I've moved since then and so have some of the teachers. I don't know how to get in touch with them. What can I *do*? I don't want to carry this guilt the rest of my life."

"Jill," her pastor counseled her, "it's right that you should feel as you do. Sin is sin. But God knows your heart. You did that cheating—wrong as it was—before you became a Christian. That sin was part of the load the Lord Jesus paid for. He doesn't want *you* to go on carrying it.

"Oh, Pastor," she sighed in relief, "Thank you, I *see* it. Can I thank the Lord right now for taking that guilt all away?"

As she prayed, the Holy Spirit gave Jill the assurance that her past sin was indeed forgiven. Peace replaced the feelings of guilt.

When it is possible, we do need to deal directly with the people involved. But, as Jill's pastor told her, God understands all about our feelings, our motives, and our opportunities to seek forgiveness. It's not His will that a believer be burdened by sins of the past that the blood of Jesus Christ has already dealt with.

But sometimes it is possible to "go back" and apologize and ask forgiveness.

During a crusade in George Beverly Shea's home town, Winchester, Ontario, Canada, I witnessed this heartwarming scene at the close of one of the meetings: a fine-looking woman approached Mr. Shea and said, "I was your third grade teacher." He greeted her warmly, then she told him, "I still have the letter you wrote me after your family moved away from here. You asked me to forgive you for not always being obedient in class."

"Why, bless you, Ma'am," said Mr. Shea, "I've been asking people to forgive me ever since."

Step Number Two

Confession on its own is not enough.

"My husband makes generous confession of all his sins and faults," Grace complained, "but that's the end of it. The confession is expected to take care of everything. He then looks to the rest of us to do the changing, to adapt to his behavior and accept it. *He lives by rules he makes himself*," she added in frustration.

The next word is *REPENT.*

In the first recorded Christian sermon (Acts 2) Peter makes no bones about what the real issue is. When, convicted by his message, the hearers cried, "Brethren, what shall we do?" (v. 37), Peter did not give any options. He said, "Repent...." Those who did repent—"about three thousand"—gave ample evidence that their repentance was genuine; the rest of Acts 2 makes that clear.

It's impossible for people to see into our hearts and tell that we have repented of our sin. John the Baptist, never noted for mincing words, exhorted his hearers to "Bear fruit worthy of repentance." Not just any "fruit"; it's the change, the improved behavior and attitudes and values that speaks for our professed repentance.

I was never sure for a while just what my own mother thought about my conversion (later I learned that she had as a child known what it was to be associated with Christians and probably had become a believer, although she never openly said so). One evening I chanced to overhear a conversation between Mother and a neighbor.

The neighbor had apparently asked Mother what had happened to me: "She's getting religious," was what I heard of the conversation. And my mother answered, "I don't know all about it. But I know this, she's a better daughter than she was before." I didn't know how to construe "better"; I didn't know what my mother had observed that caused her to make the statement. I did thank the Lord for letting me know that by some means my "fruit of repentance" was showing. I was the first in my family to accept Christ openly, and it was a great responsibility. It was so easy to fail, to give someone at home cause to say, "And *you're* a Christian!"

Hearing my mother's admission gave me a good feeling. Somehow, by my attitude or behavior or my new interests, Mother had observed in me something that recommended my new-found faith and made her my champion. This gave me confidence that I was really, to a degree, living a changed life.

But first, I had to come to the place of repentance, a facing up to the fact that I was a sinner in need of a Savior. Repentance must always precede confession.

The end result of repentance and confession is, normally, a changed life, genuine repentance "fruit."

7

You Call *That* Forgiveness?

Excusing is no substitute for forgiving.

NOT EVERYTHING THAT calls itself forgiveness *is* forgiveness. Here is one example:

I was driving along a Los Angeles freeway enroute to a dinner appointment. In the passenger seat was a friend, Myrna, from out of state. Hardly had we entered the freeway when she began to give me directions—and she had never been to the place we were going to!

Never overconfident about "how to get there," this time I did know. However, her constant heckling rattled me, and when she said authoritatively, "You should take the next exit," I did. That was the beginning of my getting really lost. "I'll stop at a service station and ask," I assured Myrna. At which point she took over: "Get into the other lane"; "Don't forget you're looking for a gas station," and more of the same. Finally, having spotted a gas station, I was pulling into a left turn lane, when she said, *"There's* a gas station!" At that, I blew my top. *"Myrna,"* I said between clenched teeth, *"I know a gas station when I see one!"*

Immediately I felt contrite. I hated myself for what I had just said. I reached over and took one of her hands and said, "I shouldn't have said that. *Please* forgive me, Myrna."

"Oh, that's alright," she said in a soothing tone. "You're tired. Maybe you had a hard day."

I found myself *so* irritated by her response, and I didn't understand why I felt as I did.

The very next day I had opportunity to discuss the situation with a psychologist colleague. "Why did I feel so angry?" I asked after I had explained the circumstances.

"Well," he replied, "for one thing, your friend didn't forgive you; she *excused* you."

"That was better than nothing," I countered, "so why did it irk me so?"

"Her tone as you described it, as well as her words, had in it, 'You poor dear, what else can I expect from you? Now, *I* would never verbally abuse anyone as you did. But I'm big enough to overlook it in you.' There's a superciliousness in such so-called forgiveness that leaves the person feeling *not* forgiven, but put down; demeaned."

"And she called that forgiveness," I said.

How glad we can all be that when God forgives us, He does not merely excuse us. He always knows "what kind of day we've had"; but that is immaterial. In response to our plea for forgiveness, God *forgives.*

We would do well to think seriously of how *what we say* will affect the one who asks us for forgiveness.

When We Fall Off the Pedestal

Another aspect of forgiveness is that we feel someone has done something that calls for forgiveness when in truth it's just that we have too high expectations of the person. For some reason we see the person in a "perfect" role; we then have unrealistic ideas of what this person should be and do.

Janet has this problem. Cindy, her best friend, said to her one day, "Jan, when you like a person you put burdens on that person."

"Why—I don't know what you mean," Janet stammered.

"I mean just this, Jan: *nobody is perfect.* Yet you put people up on a pedestal; then when they fall off, you get all upset. You need to learn that *nobody* is going to fulfill your expectations of them *all the time.* Oh, I don't mean to hurt you, Jan," she said solicitously.

"It's OK. I'd never thought about what you've just said. And I would rather have you tell me than someone else, Cindy. I'll try to watch it."

"What I'm really saying—and it's for me as well as you—is that we have no right to set the standards for other people. God has done that. It's to Him we are answerable. You know the verse that tells us, 'A man stands or falls to his own master'—that's what I mean," Cindy further explained. "So when we feel a friend has failed us and should come and ask forgiveness, it's good to ask, 'Whose standard has she come short of?' I can't promise you that I'm not going to fall short of what you expect of me, Jan."

In a lighter tone—as though she had gotten the message—Jan replied, "Anybody but you, Cindy. I don't think I could stand it if *you* let me down."

"Well, just keep in mind that I'm not going to be continually asking you for forgiveness for behavior that doesn't measure up to your ideal of me, Jan. And nobody else is either. So I hope you will keep that in mind. You won't get hurt so often if you do."

There is a standard by which we can judge *ourselves:*

He has told you, O man, what is good; and what does the Lord require of you but to do justice, to love kindness, and to walk humbly with your God? (Micah 6:8).

Meeting a Neurotic Need

Not all petitions for forgiveness are justified.

There are people who go around apologizing and asking forgiveness for nothing at all. They appear to have such a low self-image that they feel they must be "doing something wrong" all the time; therefore they must be asking for forgiveness from anybody who is around. It's

69

hard to feel comfortable around such people for any length of time.

To respond to what would seem to be the person's neurotic need to hear himself saying, "Please forgive me," by simply saying, "I forgive you," is of little help to the individual. He needs someone to take time with him and help him to understand what he's doing to himself.

Fred said, concerning someone like this, "I sometimes feel I should do something to cause Harry to offend me, so I could act normal when he comes around asking to forgive him."

We are never called on by the Lord to apologize for our existence. This is demeaning to our Creator in whose image we were made. For us as Christians, without "thinking more highly of ourselves than we should" as Paul exhorts (Romans 12:3), we can glory in what we are *in Christ*.

There will generally be enough things we really need to ask forgiveness for, without manufacturing some in order to meet a neurotic need.

We cannot go through life with a kind of conscience geiger counter, seeking to unearth, "Whom have I hurt today?" We *can* ask the Lord to make us sensitive. This is well expressed in an old hymn:

"If I have wounded any soul today,
If I have caused one foot to go astray,
If I have walked in my own willful way,
Dear Lord — forgive."

Asking More Than God Asks

Some people, in the area of forgiveness, promote themselves to being God in the lives of others.

Alice's mother was such a person. To be sure, she was motivated by her love for her daughter. Alice's husband, Joe, had been anything but a good husband. While Alice was not a complainer, her mother knew her daughter was unhappy. Then one day Alice phoned from the distant state she and Joe had moved to. "Mom," she exclaimed, "know what? *Joe accepted the Lord* — and, oh, everything

70

is *so* different!" The phone line couldn't cloud the joy in Alice's voice as she exulted in what was happening in their lives.

But on the other end of the line was no reciprocal joy. In a cynical voice, the mother responded, "I'll believe it when I see it. It'll take more than this phone call to convince me that there's any change in *that* man!"

"Oh, *Mother,*" Alice replied, "I thought you would be overjoyed."

A "Hmmm" was the response.

"What *will* it take, Mom, for you to believe Joe—to forgive him?"

"*Here's* what it will take, Alice. You make Joe sit right down and write me *himself,* confessing all the wrong he's done and all the unhappiness he's brought on you. I want it in his words, *not yours.* I want to be sure he has really repented and is really a changed man. Maybe *then* I'll forgive him. But he'll have to *prove* himself!"

Write a statement of confession and contrition to your *in-laws?* Isn't that asking more of a penitent than God in heaven does? Nowhere in the Bible do we read, "Thou shalt confess to thy mother-in-law and therefore prove thyself."

Part of the "proof" was that Joe, rather than resenting his mother-in-law's demand, complied with it. Nevertheless she maintained her "I'll wait and see" attitude while asserting how big-hearted she was in "forgiving" her son-in-law.

The couple's happy life in the years that followed was ample evidence that the letter had been written with a true motive, not just to pacify a mother-in-law. Meanwhile she, herself, lost out on the joy which accompanies a genuinely forgiving spirit.

Forgiveness That Costs Nothing

There's another kind of put-down that poses as forgiveness.

Becky was visiting back in the town where she had gone to school. She took the opportunity to go and see a former schoolmate and ask her forgiveness for deliberately snaring the other's boyfriend when they were both adolescents.

"Oh, it's you, Becky," Lydia greeted her. "It's been a long time."

"Yes, I know," Becky agreed. "Even so, I had to take this chance to hunt you up. Remember how mad you were at me for taking Ron away from you in junior high?"

"Of course, I do."

"Well, that's why I've come. I want to say I'm sorry. It was a very unkind thing to do deliberately. I would like to ask you to forgive me. Will you, Lydia?"

"Forgive you?" She stood surveying Becky for a few seconds, then repeated in an airy tone, "*Forgive* you? Well, I *suppose* I can. If it means all that much to you to hear me say 'I forgive you,' then I'm saying it, 'I forgive you, Rebekah.'"

Becky, meanwhile, fervently wished she had never come.

"After all," Lydia tacked on, "it doesn't cost me anything."

Becky left without further words but under her breath she was saying, 'You call *that* forgiving?"

True Forgiveness Cancels

"Forgiveness" is a special word. It's allied in our mind with God and everything that is good.

There's a *completeness* about true forgiveness. When, therefore, we are granted some kind of conditional or "probationary forgiveness," although we may not be able to put it into words, we feel cheated. This does something to our spirit. (It's almost as if we had come upon Jesus being lacking in compassion.)

Indeed, compassion is the missing element when we don't or won't quite forgive. Compassion for the one who has wronged us will enable us, with *God's help*, to grant the forgiveness that wholly cancels the offense. That is true forgiveness.

Some time ago I sat in on a demonstration of a computer. Being totally unmechanical, I did not expect to grasp what the demonstrater was teaching. But, since I like to learn new things, and "computerese" is a modern language, I knew I would get some benefit from the time spent.

I learned of "default messages" and "motivation codes." The meaningless (to me) phrases swirled around, most of them going in one ear and out the other because of my lack of background for listening to them. Suddenly I perked up and listened intently, as the instructor repeated, "If you don't like a line you've done, just enter a *C* for cancel."

Wow, I thought, *I wonder if that man knows the implications of what he just said.* I heard no more as my mind moved into a different gear.

Canceled. As though it had never been programmed in in the first place.

Blotted out — as if it had never been!

How can I ever thank this person for phrasing it as he did, so that even I could comprehend this piece of computerese?

Canceled. That's forgiveness.

To my mind came the words of the Lord Jesus Christ, "Now you are clean" (as though the dirt had never been); not through a keypunched *C;* not through the application of a chalkboard eraser; but "because of the word which I have spoken," declared the Savior of the world (John 15:3).

God the Son redeemed us — canceled out the sin — by "blotting out the handwriting of ordinances that was against us...nailing it to His cross" (Colossians 2:14 KJV).

The computer's *C* can cancel an operator's error. Only God can cancel sin.

God's *C* stands for *C*hrist Jesus who came into the world to save sinners.

He breaks the power of canceled sin;
He sets the captive free;
His blood can make the foulest clean,
His blood availed for me.

Charles Wesley

Destroying the Evidence

The last word in repentance is *quit*, forsake the sin.

73

Just as surely, there is a last *act* in forgiving, if it is to have credibility. We need to rid ourselves of everything we have hung on to with the intent of indicting someone. There can be but questionable forgiveness and little chance for forgetting when we deliberately file something that can be used against the person whom we purport to have forgiven.

Tom had suffered at the hands of a business partner who had connived against him. The partner, Bill, realized how wrong he had been, asked Tom's forgiveness and made restitution. Nevertheless, Tom continued to harbor ill feelings even after he had said he forgave Bill. Some months later he came to see how destructive hanging on to an old grudge really was. He sought out his former partner and confessed that he had not really forgiven him until that time. "But that was not the end of it," Tom relates. "I went home and dug out all the stuff I had accumulated against Bill — and I had quite a dossier on him! It was not until I had gathered up every single item and burned it all, that I really felt at peace with Bill — and with God."

Tom forgave, then put the past behind him. As long as he retained his folio, he was nurturing and perpetuating the offense, keeping the door open for remembering what was best forgotten.

Getting rid of the evidence is doing, on the human level, what God does for us when we repent and seek His forgiveness. We read "Thou hast cast all my sins behind Thy back" (Isaiah 38:17, KJV), and "You will tread our sins beneath your feet; You will throw them into the depths of the ocean!" (Micah 7:19, TLB). As I heard one Christian say, "If the devil goes after my sins, he'll *drown*."

"I will remember your sin no more."

That is forgiveness.

8
Right—
But Unforgiving

*It's hard to forgive the person who
won't let you "be right."*

GRACE AND MARCIA came bounding into the kitchen
after school.

"Mom," said Grace, half out of breath. "Know what? It's
just seventeen days till school's out."

"You're wrong, Grace. It's *nineteen* days," Marcia
corrected her.

"I'm not wrong. You are," Grace insisted, and turning to
her mother she plead, "Tell her she's wrong, Mom, since I
know I'm right."

The harangue went on till their mother lost patience and
banished them to their rooms to do homework. Grace
muttered as she reluctantly obeyed, "I know she's wrong. I
know she's wrong."

Grace is a girl who finds it impossible to forgive others
because she cannot emotionally afford to be wrong about
anything. And the very act of saying, "Please forgive me,"
is an admission that she is at least partially responsible for
the hostility between them. This would undermine her own

image of herself.

"Having to be right" is death to ongoing good relationships. It hurts the one who insists he is right and creates a feeling of inferiority on the part of the one who must always give in. Those who must always be right project a Thank-God-I'm-not-like-other-men attitude. They see no reason why they should ever forgive or ask forgiveness.

Sometimes in as harmless a thing as playing a game, this trait shows up. And not just with children. I once saw a family being pulled in three directions in the course of a game that two elderly in-laws were engaged in. The wife's mother and the husband's father, both in their seventies, were engrossed in a quiz-type game having to do with world geography. The location of a river was the point at issue. The mother-in-law insisted, "It's in South Africa."

"No. You're *wrong,*" argued the father-in-law, "I know it's in *South America!*"

If the scene had stopped there it would have been a normal little interaction such as occurs in any family. But this man and woman hung on to his and her point of view and wouldn't yield an inch. Rather than an enjoyable pastime, the game became a contest of wills. Finally, the distraught wife appealed to her husband, "*Please stop your father;* he's getting my mother all worked up." The equally frustrated husband answered, "Why don't you get your mother off my dad's back?" And it turned into a family fracas.

Silly? Yes, but not too uncommon.

And how often have you listened to something like this:

"I tell you it was a Friday," asserts one person.

"You're *wrong.* I distinctly recall that it was a *Tuesday,*" the other counters, and the two go at it like a terrier with a bone. No matter that whatever it was they're arguing about is in the past, that neither can do anything about it now, and that it may have been trivial even when it happened. Neither will drop the subject in the interest of the other's feelings.

Why was it important in either of these instances that one be right? Nothing was to be gained by it, and certainly a lot was lost. Their love for one another was forgotten; the

Christian grace of "in honor preferring one another" (Romans 12:10) was ignored. For the time being all that each was concerned with was proving "I am right."

Having to be right is a childish trait, pardonable in a little kid, obnoxious in a big kid. It says out loud, "I can't stand to have someone else appear in a better light than I do." This is generally believed to be an outer sign of inner deep insecurity, the low self-concept that causes one to see himself as less informed than other people, less to be looked up to as an authority on certain things. He is, therefore, almost belligerent in his attempts to prove the very opposite, that he is *right*.

"When I'm right, make me easy to live with," prayed Peter Marshall.

What did he mean?

For one thing, my being right is usually predicated on your being wrong. So right, which we assume to be a good and positive quality, can be both negative and destructive of peace and harmony. Someone who must always be right is never prepared to say, "I could have been mistaken; please forgive me." And it's difficult for him to change.

Should he recognize the trait for what it is and want to change, a good first step might be to ask himself these questions:

In the things I argue about, what difference does it make who is right?

Is it worth it after I prove that I am right? What do I get out of it?

Am I getting all worked up—expending emotional energy—on something quite irrelevant?

In a week, or a month, or a year, what will it matter who was right?

Gradually this approach can lead away from childish attitudes and behavior to more mature judgment when one is tempted to prove "I am right."

Joe discovered that healthy relationships are more to be desired than being right.

"It used to be the biggest thing in the world to me to show that I was right," he admits. "But I sometimes wondered why afterwards I felt so lousy inside. It just wasn't all that satisfying, believe me. Then one night when I had been arguing about the previous season's hockey champions, I found myself thinking, *Why am I so tense and hostile? Here's Dave, relaxed and apparently a whole lot happier than I am. Why don't I forget this argument — let the thing go, for once?* So I said, 'Hey, Dave, I think this is a silly argument I started. It's getting us nowhere.'"

"Just what I was thinking," Dave answered with a smile. "C'mon, let's go shoot some baskets."

"And from that night," Joe tells, "I've asked the Lord to help me overcome that awful desire to be always right. It's paying off. I find I have more friends and better relationships with people in general than I used to have when I was 'right.'"

Joe exercised his prerogative of choice, opting for feeling good himself which then made for a good chain reaction. He realized a greater triumph than "being right" had ever brought him. He gained the quiet joy that comes when we deliberately put the other person's feelings above our desire to be proven right.

How to Lose Friends

We tend to suppose that our being right will make us look big in the eyes of other people. Generally, we could not be more wrong, for the very reverse is more often true. We end up looking very small — and the loser becomes the winner!

"There he goes again; always has to be right," said Harry's friends in some disgust. They had heard him take on another of their bowling team at the snack bar — something about the merits of regular or diet soda.

"I, for one, am *getting tired of it,*" John complained. "Who needs *him* for a friend?"

"Yet apart from that one irritating trait he's a nice guy. I *like* Harry," Pete admitted. "If he just didn't have to turn every little thing into an argument that creates bad feelings — just to prove he's right."

So Harry pays a high price for his "being right." People shy away from him because whatever subject is brought up, he's sure to argue, and his last words could be counted on to be "You're wrong." Hurt feelings and the lack of consideration were too high a price to pay for friendship with Harry. He will do well to think about something the Apostle Paul wrote about being a know-it-all.

"We know in part" (1 Corinthians 13:9); Paul had no illusions that he knew everything about everything. It was in this context that he wrote, "When I was a child, I spoke as a child...but when I became a man, I put away childish things." As we have mentioned earlier, having to be right is a distinctively childish attitude.

Jennifer said of a former friend, "Sarah challenged every little thing I said. I found myself having to monitor my words when I was around her. It was like walking on eggs. Before I spoke I would find myself thinking, *If I say _____, how will it affect our relationship? Will it spark another tense, 'I'm right, you're wrong' sequence?* So, although I like her, I had to give up that friendship." She gave this example:

"Sarah was talking about the raise in candy prices.

"'I know,' I agreed. 'I can remember paying just twelve cents for a Peter Paul candy bar, back in '74,' and Sarah jumped me with, 'No. You're *wrong*, Jennifer. That was '73. We paid fifteen cents in 1974,' and she was off on a harangue to prove she was right."

Both young women are Christians. But you couldn't have proved it by Sarah! As I listened to Jennifer's account of the argument I thought, *If I'm going to jeopardize my Christian testimony, let it be over something more significant than the price of a Peter Paul candy bar in 1974!* Also, I pondered, who is so rich in friends that she can afford to alienate even one by such childish behavior? To say nothing of how such conduct looks to the non-Christians standing by. They may be caused to think that this is how most or all Christians act toward each other.

How then, can we go about helping to answer our own prayer, "When I am right, make me easy to live with"?

One way is by not permitting ourselves the doubtful luxury of proving we are right.

Another, by letting the person appear right when there's nothing at stake, when there is nothing to be gained or lost by "who is right."

Confusing the Issue

Those of us who must be right all the time too often confuse the point at issue with the person himself.

"If only Mom would say something like, 'You could be mistaken, you know,'" Emily sighed. "But no, she has to say, 'Emily, you're wrong'; not what I've done or said but me—myself—*I* am wrong. I feel so put down all the time."

Saying to someone, "You're wrong," implies just that. Not "your information, your opinion, your words, or your behavior is wrong (therefore unacceptable)," but you, yourself, are wrong.

The statement may be made with good intentions, but by the very nature of it, the hearer senses the hostility and reacts accordingly.

Some Bible verses that speak to this matter are, "Be not wise in your own conceits" (Romans 12:16), "Love is not arrogant" (1 Corinthians 13:4), and the Golden Rule in Matthew 7:12. Another helpful portion is 2 Timothy 3:16, "All Scripture is inspired by God and profitable for teaching, for reproof...." *Reproof,* telling us we need to change. This is *God* speaking to us. And, unlike our friends and acquaintances who tell us we're wrong (reprove us) then leave us with hurt feelings and no help, God goes on to help us change. His Word is good for *correction,* for *instruction in righteousness.* As we heed what God is saying, we can overcome our weaknesses and our traits which irritate other people...such as having to be right all the time.

Jesus Did Not Have to Be Right

Sheldon, in the classic, *In His Steps,* repeatedly poses the question, "What would Jesus do?"

Throughout His life on earth Jesus could have always had the last word and won every argument. He could have shut off any and all who dared to try to prove Him "wrong." He is the only one who ever lived who could have closed out every discussion and dispute with an irrefutable,

"I *know*." He did know, not only the facts but even all that lay behind them, in every situation. But He did not stoop to gain satisfaction by putting people down. Take the Mary and Martha incident (Luke 10:38-42). Martha comes with her querulous, "Lord, do you not care that my sister has left me to do all the serving alone? Then tell her to help me" (v. 40).

The Lord Jesus might have reprimanded her. Rather, He quieted her with His, "Martha, Martha, you are worried and bothered about so many things; but only a few things are necessary...Mary has chosen the good part, which shall not be taken away from her" (v. 41,42). No put-down, just an explanation of priorities.

Jesus could have made many a person look foolish, absurd. He could have caused some to crawl from His presence licking what was left of their damaged ego. Jesus was too big for that. He came to demonstrate for us what God is like. And God is not condescending. He is not small or petty. He does not have to demean His creatures in order to prove that He is right. He is considerate of our sensitivities. "He knows our frame" (Psalm 103:14).

On the cross, the Lord Jesus Christ could have reminded His followers who stood by that He was right: "*I told* you I would be crucified." He didn't. He was occupied in praying for those who had shouted, "Crucify Him!" He saved His dying breath for, "Father, *forgive* them."

How can we best thank Him for that so great forgiveness that includes you and me? By caring for all kinds of people; by showing a forgiving spirit; and, with God's help, rising above the need to "be right."

9

The Handle Is Showing

Why is it that we have instant, 100 percent recall of the sins and faults of others?

MARGARET IS A good wife, mother, in-law, neighbor, church member and friend. Among her fine qualities is her willingness to forgive. The words "I forgive you" seem to come easily to her lips.

But is she all that forgiving?

It took a discerning friend, Alice, to help Margaret reconsider her airy kind of "forgiveness."

One day, when it was appropriate, Alice began gently, "There's something I feel I should mention but I don't want to hurt your feelings, Margaret."

"Go right ahead. I promise not to feel hurt — or, even if I am, I'll forgive..."

"There!" Alice interrupted. "That is exactly what I want to talk about. You've given me a real opening."

Margaret smiled her encouragement, and Alice plunged in with, "You're so good at saying 'I forgive you,' but what do you mean? Why is it that later you always bring up the very things you've said you've forgiven? Seems to me that real forgiveness takes care of that."

Margaret looked incredulous, then she stammered, *"I*

don't do that, do I? I wasn't aware—I didn't know—I certainly don't want to be that kind of person." She paused then added, "I'll think seriously about what you've told me, Alice." Then, some of her breeziness returning, she said, "Thank you—I *think*."

The two parted, but later in the day Margaret phoned Alice. "Know what I've been thinking about? Something I used to hear my grandfather say—he got it from an old Indian friend. Here it is: 'I'll bury the hatchet but I'll keep the handle sticking up.' And I think, 'Have I been doing *that?*'"

It often takes the loving and insightful rebuke of someone who cares for us, to make us see ourselves as we are and to determine to change.

Why is partial forgiveness not forgiveness at all?

One reason is that when someone says, "I forgive you" we generally take it at face value.

How could Margaret's friends and associates know that what she had "forgiven" would later be brought up, possibly held against them? They would not suspect that the "forgiveness" could be revoked at their next real or fancied offense against her, in the manner of a STOP PAYMENT.

It would be as though Margaret had offered to pay the debt of a friend who was unable to pay it and who was deeply troubled about it. The check arrives. The friend takes it to Margaret's bank. The teller punches the account number into the computer and immediately there's a problem. The teller excuses herself and finds her superior. They return to the computer and the delay is explained. "I'm sorry, but we have a 'Stop' on this check." Incredulous, the friend makes her way out of the bank she had entered so hopefully. Margaret had issued the check but for some reason had stopped payment on it.

By contrast, I heard a conference speaker state, "I asked God for grace to forgive a certain person, and to help me *forget*. And," she declared, "I distinctly remember the very time and place where I forgot."

My mind did a double take over this contradiction in terms. What *was* the woman saying? How can one "remember forgetting"?

What was she saying? "As far as is humanly possible I have forgiven, and from this moment I will give no place to the memory of the incident."

Only God can totally forgive and forget. His Word tells us (Isaiah 43:25) "I, even I, am He that blotteth out thy transgressions...and will not remember thy sins" (KJV).

I'm not discounting this speaker's experience. However, I have personally found that it is not wise to set out to forget traumatic experiences that involve forgiving another person. "Trying to forget," the making a dedicated project of forgiving, in itself surfaces memories.

We are not God. We cannot, at will, blot out the entire past. In fact, there is growing evidence that all we have ever seen or heard, all that has registered in our mind is permanently stored in that marvelous God-given computer, our brain.

How then can we hope to bury the hatchet — handle and all? Yet God has bidden us forgive. Praise be to His name, He never fails to provide us with the inner strength and grace to obey His commands.

A willingness to obey often results in God's sending just the right person across our way to help us. Florence, for example, was ruining her life by her bitter spirit toward her mother. One day a friend, Louise, was rhapsodizing about her new, solid relationship with her daughter-in-law.

"It's fine for you to talk about forgiveness and all," Florence snapped. "You don't have a mother like mine. Your mother didn't break up your marriage. Oh, I've tried the forgiveness bit" she said in a bragging tone, "but it doesn't work. I'm not like you, I guess."

A faraway look came into Louise's eyes. "Oh, Florence," she sighed, "If you only *knew*. I fought God about forgiving my daughter-in-law; I gave Him all the arguments, every reason why He couldn't have meant me when He said we should forgive. My daughter-in-law hated me and she showed it every way she knew how. I wasn't about to be the one to do any forgiving. No matter how I tried to make and keep some kind of truce between us, I came out the loser, the comic-strip mother-in-law. I tried fighting her; I threw out what I knew God's Word said about loving my enemy—for that she was. I thought we'd never..."

"Tell me," Florence chipped in, "tell me what happened? I see you two together and nobody would ever believe you had been *enemies.*"

"I know," a warm smile played around Louise's face. Her eyes shone.

"It's wonderful," she said. "How did it come about? Well, all I can say is that the Lord was better to me than I deserve. One day when I was feeling desperate and totally helpless about the situation with Melissa, I seemed to hear Him say, 'It's up to you. You are the older woman. You should be the wiser. Look inside yourself.' I listened. I did try to take an objective look at myself—but, do you want to hear all this, Florence?"

"Yes, yes, go on, please."

"Well, as I prayed and searched my heart, I began to recognize ways in which I could have been alienating my daughter-in-law. I determined to take the responsibility for changing things. If Melissa's not going to change—and that seems hardly likely at the moment—then with God's help I will. She is the mother of my grandchildren as well as being my son's wife. She is part of my family."

Florence was listening intently, without comment.

"I began to treat Melissa as though she were a kind and thoughtful daughter-in-law. I looked for little things in her behavior that I could praise her for. Before that time, I had only picked on her flaws. At first, she was understandably suspicious of my motives when I would take her a little present, or offer to help her with the ironing or such. She had been resistant to any of my offers, with an I-can-do-it-myself-thank-you attitude. But she began to mellow. Oh, it wasn't overnight. Her old attitudes (and, I suspect mine from her point of view) reared up from time to time, and I felt I was losing the battle.

"But again and again would come to me the wisdom of the Lord, 'A soft answer turns away wrath,' and gradually our relationship completely changed."

Florence sat for a moment in silence, then, jumping up she said, "So it *can happen.*"

"Yes," agreed Louise. "And you can be sure I'll be praying with you about the problem with your mother."

It can happen.

I don't know how God accomplishes this work of grace in our hearts. I don't know how He restores relationships through transformed attitudes. I just know that He does. I would expect that the process is tied into our obedience to Matthew 5:44, "Pray for those who despitefully use you." We cannot honestly pray for someone who has injured us and at the same time hang on to anger and resentment and continue to withhold forgiveness.

Whatever the hurt, it is included in the "pray for them." Notice how serious were the offenses mentioned in the verse: the people were *enemies,* they have *cursed* us, *hated* us, *persecuted,* and otherwise *despitefully used us.*

God knew that there would always be some around who would counsel us to retaliate: "How could they do that to you? Get even with them. They deserve to suffer." But God says love them and pray for them. His word should be enough for us. And when we sincerely obey, and pray for those who have injured us, God does enable us to have a forgiving spirit toward them.

It's not easy. It's not even a human response; it's superhuman, one of the "all things" we can accomplish "through Christ who strengthens us." Nor is this high plateau reached in one giant step; it's a process of believing God's Word and practicing it in ways that cut across the grain of our natural inclination.

Putting the Past Behind

I am indebted to a psychologist friend, Dr. George Martindale, for the following insights regarding forgiving and forgetting:

> Our inability to forget need not prevent us from enjoying life to the full, since we can learn to model our behavior after Christ's. That is to say, we can refuse to dwell in the past, even in the light of what has happened in the past. We can love ourselves and others *in the present.*

Actually, doing this can make love for others more meaningful. If we can love only when we have forgotten the unpleasantness or injury, what does such "love" mean? It's when we can love even though we are in a state of full awareness of past transgressions on the other person's part that we are truly emulating the love of Christ for us. This attitude produces the fruit of the Spirit, *joy*.

The question, How can I forget? is intimately associated with our behavior and related to our individual differences of learning and experience. By our conscious acts of love in the present, we are exhibiting behavior that is inconsistent and incompatible with unpleasant memories of the past. Such behavior will increase the probabilities of our being able to forget the past and its ills.

There's a sense in which such behavior and reactions as Dr. Martindale refers to is akin to "heaping coals of fire on the person's head." Almost certainly, if such behavior is not in line with what they normally view in you, the "forgiven" might conceivably be thoroughly confused. This brings to mind a slogan I saw a number of times on an outdoor bulletin board as I drove past a church in Pasadena. In bold letters it suggested,

LOVE YOUR ENEMIES — CONFUSE THEM

If these one-time enemies are sufficiently confused by your changed attitude and behavior, it could be that this will present a strategic opportunity for Christian witness. For, if we are honest with ourselves, we all have to admit that it is "not I, but Christ in me" when by His grace we act even a little bit like the One we profess to love and serve.

I recently read in a church bulletin a prayer that went something like this: "Thank You, Lord, that I can't always forget, for remembering helps me to keep from repeating the very things for which I have asked forgiveness."

When the Church Will Not Forgive

Miriam's father had been a deacon in the church as long as she could remember. Her mother headed women's committees, sang in the choir, and represented the church at denominational conventions. Miriam's parents were, in essence, a pillar-of-the-church couple. Their other children had followed along in the same fine pattern. It was Miriam, their youngest, who caused them to hang their heads in shame: she had rejected both their teaching and example; she lived by her own rules. That is, until one night when it seemed that all the prayers for Miriam had descended on her head and she came to church, openly expressed her desire to change, and prayed the penitent's prayer, "God be merciful to me, a sinner" (Luke 18:13).

How well I recall that occasion ("Miriam" is not her real name). With others in our church I had prayed fervently for this young woman, and now my heart was glad because of the joyous answer God had given.

Ours was a warm church family, compassionate, caring, and generally willing to reach out with a helping hand, especially to one who had just taken a step of faith toward the Lord. But not this time. There seemed to be a tacit let's-wait-and-see-if-she-really-means-it attitude toward Miriam and her conversion (or restoration, as it may well have been). She was going to have to prove herself before she would be accepted. The church was keeping the handle sticking up.

The continued censure on the part of some members of our church — their wait-and-see withholding of acceptance — was at least partially responsible for Miriam's gradually reverting to her old ways.

I need to say in defense of that congregation that they didn't know how to handle such a situation (which doesn't say much for a church given to helping at rescue missions and such outreach places). They did not want this young woman around their own sons and daughters; some didn't know how to talk to her, what to *say* so they failed her rather than risk being uncomfortable around her. We surely needed greater emphasis on the incident of Christ's dealing with the woman at the well, for if ever there was a model of how to deal with one who comes into our midst from an unsavory background, we have it in John 4:7-42.

As for cataloging sins and dispensing forgiveness

accordingly, how can we reconcile such an approach with Psalm 103:2-3a:

"Bless the Lord, O my soul, and forget none of His benefits; Who pardons all your iniquities..."

The first of David's long list of blessings: forgiveness for *all* our sins, not for selected "acceptable ones." God's forgiveness package includes for the repentant, remission of every sin. Burying the hatchet — handle and all.

To you, the one who has been wronged, the one who has to *do* the forgiving, let me say, "God will not do your forgiving for you." But He has given to every one of us the perfect example (His Son, our Savior); and He has given us "the tools to do the job."

It won't ever be easy.

It will take time.

It calls for a willingness to forgive.

It will take the power of the Holy Spirit at work in the heart.

Ultimately, you *can* find yourself able to forgive, to bury the hatchet — with never a handle showing.

10
The Spoilers

No one is a confirmed failure until he cannot forgive another for being successful.

JEALOUSY IS A spoiler. Like the "little foxes that spoil the vine" (Song of Solomon 2:15), it can hinder or prevent the development of a forgiving spirit.

"I might be able to forgive Mabel," Frieda said to a neighbor, "if she just wasn't *so irritatingly good* at everything."

"So what's so bad about being good at doing things?" the neighbor interrupted.

"Nothing, I suppose. And it's not Mabel's success that bugs me; it's how her always being successful makes me feel."

"Then you would feel better if Mabel would fail?" probed Anne, the neighbor.

"No," protested Frieda, "I don't mean that at all." She shook herself and added, "I don't know what I mean. It's just hard for me to have good feelings about her, to forgive her for being what I can't ever seem to be myself."

Frieda's ill-feelings toward Mabel may have started as a "little fox" of dislike but, fed by Frieda's dwelling on the subject, the dislike blossomed into an inability to forgive.

Jealousy also takes many forms.

"I haven't a jealous bone in my body," insisted Jane's mother-in-law over and over. But her actions belied her words. Jealous of her son's happiness with his wife, she went to all extremes to drive a wedge between them. The unsuspecting son, Tom, fell into her trap. He began to see his wife as a bit paranoid when she tried to make him understand what his mother's behavior was doing to her. "Mom's all right. You're imagining things, Jane," he would respond. And the marriage had little chance of success.

Actually, Tom's mother could not forgive the girl who had "taken him from her," and she made up her mind she would get him away from his wife, back to herself.

"Jealousy is as cruel as the grave," the Bible tells us (Song of Solomon 8:6). It's cruel toward the person it is directed at. Also jealousy can eat at the heart of the one who gives it room.

A Step Beyond

Envy, first cousin of jealousy, goes beyond that emotion to a kind of hatred. Envy says, "Not only do I not like you being or having a certain something, I want it for myself at your expense." Generally the person will go to all lengths to attempt the other's downfall in the belief that it will build himself up.

A few days ago, a friend of mine was showing a group of church members a painting she had just completed. The women made nice comments and congratulated the budding artist on her work. Later, one of those women confided, "I said all the nice things like the rest of the group about Marion's painting. But I was not being honest. I didn't want her to get all that praise. I was wishing *I* was the one they were ooh-ing and aah-ing over. I hate that in myself, but I don't know what to do about it."

There's hope for this woman. In admitting her feelings, she was doing something to attack the spoiler while it was still little. From that point she could ask the Lord to help her; she could also go to the woman and confess her negative feelings. Rather than feeding the little fox, she would be starving it.

If we would admit it, we all have some envious moments. It's often easier to "weep with those who weep" (though we wouldn't want the problem that's causing the weeping) than to "rejoice with those who rejoice." When we find ourselves loath to genuinely enter into another's happiness, whatever the source, it's a good time to stop and question, "Is it envy that keeps me from wholeheartedly joining in the rejoicing?"

"Envy," wrote Solomon, "is rottenness of the bones" (Proverbs 14:30). And, "Who is able to stand before envy?" (27:4).

Envy is grouped with murder, sedition, witchcraft and other kindred evil in the list of "works of the flesh" (Galatians 5:19-21). We are warned that "they that do such things shall not inherit the kingdom of God."

It was out of *envy* that the chief priests and elders delivered Jesus to Pilate. And Pilate was well aware of this fact (Matthew 27:18). The hierarchy of the Jews could not tolerate it that Jesus did things they had never been able to do. He performed miracles that caused the populace to follow Him and hang on His every word. He engendered such loyalty as the envious high priest and his cohorts could never have won to themseles. Envy did its worst. Envy crucified the Lord of glory.

Many a church has been riddled by strife because of some envious member. Pastors, choir directors and the man in the pew have been "crucified" to satisfy the envious.

Martha had a fair voice. She made a certain contribution to the contralto section of her church choir. But Martha aspired to being the contralto *soloist.* When, because her voice was not up to the part, the choir director chose someone with a more suitable voice, Martha was livid, and said she would never forgive him.

"I vow I'll get that man. He can't pass me up for someone else," she determined. So she drew a few sympathizers around her and caused them to begin to feel dissatisfaction with the choir director. Then they started a whispering campaign. Vague rumors about "something in his last church," innuendos — nothing that could be traced back to Martha but which spread viciously. Gradually others lost confidence in the choir director and the outcome was that for no other reason than Martha's vindictive envy, he was asked to leave.

"Love envies not" (1 Corinthians 13:4), so love and envy cannot coexist. Therefore we need to go on a fox hunt and kill the spoiler, envy. A good place to begin is, again, with a self-examination:

Do I envy a friend's *opportunities* (which the person has taken advantage of, hence the success)?

Am I envious of another's *friends,* without considering that he who has friends must show himself friendly?

Do I envy another's *abilities*, while not being willing to develop my own?

Am I envious of another's *promotion* (for which the person has worked and proven worthy)?

Do I cast envious glances at another's nice home (for which he has saved and sacrificed)?

Am I envious of another's pleasing disposition and good relationships with other people, without questioning my own techniques of interpersonal relationships?

There will always be someone, something to envy, for the one who is envious. Almost invariably this will lead to an inability to forgive the envied person.

Gossip — A Not-So-Little-Fox

Ruth had been bad-mouthing another woman, Sue.

"Why do you have such bad feelings about Sue?" a neighbor asked, "you seem to almost hate her."

"Well, maybe you would, too," answered Ruth defensively. "She'll hardly ever listen to me. Says it's gossip and she wants no part of it. It'll be hard for me to forgive her for that."

"Must have been something to make her say that. Are you sure you're not a bit of a gossip, Ruth?"

Gossip can be a subtle spoiler.

Why does one person revel in tattling on another?

Not always is there a vicious intent. Some people are so desperately in need of attention that they will use any means to get it. And a "scoop" about someone is almost guaranteed to draw attention to the one who is peddling such information. "The words of a gossip are tempting morsels" (Proverbs 18:8, *Berkeley*).

Sally, a new Christian, was convicted of her habitual tale-bearing when she ran across the verse in Psalm 19, "Let the words of my mouth be acceptable in Thy sight, O Lord." She asked God to help her get rid of her bad habit.

Sally was wise in recognizing that gossip is not pleasing to God. In addition, she began to see for herself that, ultimately, tattling costs people their friends. And Sally was helped by reading a simple guide for preventing her from gossiping:

1. Is what I'm about to say *true?*
2. Is it *any of my business?*
3. Am I being *kind and Christ-like* in spreading it?

The Bible is more practical. While it deplores the unwise use of the tongue, warning "Behold, how great a forest is set aflame by such a small fire!" (James 3:5), it also says, "For lack of wood the fire goes out, and where there is no whisperer, contention quiets down" (Proverbs 26:20).

The Little Fox of Bitterness

"As a young pastor's wife," Betty explained, "I started out with Jim, my husband, full of ideals as to what my life would be like. I wanted to be the very best kind of minister's wife, a true help to my husband and to contribute in the church. But oh—the disillusionment! So many things have happened to make me feel bitter. Older women have belittled me, criticized me and my children to other church members. I've felt that no matter how hard I tried, I could do nothing right, never measure up to 'our last minister's wife.' Now, I've gotten so that I don't care. I'm getting so hard and calloused."

Young people frequently become bitter.

Allan's parents are fine church members, both are Sunday school teachers. The pastor speaks of them as "a couple we couldn't do without; the church wouldn't run without them." But they have a blind spot as far as their own son is concerned. He sees them as thinking more of the church than they do of him.

"Mom and Dad have time for everything and everybody but me," he told a school counselor after he had griped about their excessive loyalty to their church. "I might as well not bother to go home; they're never *there*," he said sadly. "Other guys go home and their mom listens to what they've been doing. Not my mom. She's too busy doing things for the church kids." And the weeds of bitterness get more and more entwined in Allan's heart.

Meanwhile the Bible says, "Let all bitterness be put away" (Ephesians 4:31). Both Betty, the pastor's wife, and Allan, the Sunday school teachers' son, will need help to forgive and to put away the bitterness.

Revenge Is a Spoiler

"Out of my own hurts," an older woman admitted, "I've hurt a lot of people. I've wanted revenge against them, instead of taking God's way and leaving it to Him. The result is that I've hurt people I never intended to hurt."

What is "God's way"?

"Do not judge lest you be judged yourselves" (Matthew 7:1), and "Never pay back evil for evil to anyone... Never take your own revenge..." (Romans 12:17, 19).

God is the only One who can judge justly and He has said, "Vengeance is mine; I will repay" (v. 19).

Marilyn is a teacher in a Christian school. She was guilty of wrong behavior with one of the men teachers and though she confessed to her husband and asked his forgiveness, he was adamant that she should pay for her sin. All her attempts at reconciliation deadened and finally they were legally separated. From that time on, for Marilyn, it was a series of getting a job, holding it for a short time, then being fired. Her husband, bent on revenge, would not give up. Out of his own hurts, for which he would not forgive his repentant wife, he set out to keep on hurting her.

"Where will this end?" his pastor asked the husband. "Do you plan to dog your wife's life, to be always ready to expose her and get her fired? Or, would you be willing to forgive her and leave the judging and 'repaying' up to God? You surely don't want to spend the rest of your life being a witness for the prosecution against your own wife!"

With some counseling from his pastor, the husband found it possible to deal in love rather than in judgment with his wife; the result, a happier marriage than they had formerly known.

The little foxes spoil the produce in the garden. The love of God shed abroad in the heart "kills the little foxes."

The Spoilers God Hates

God is in the *loving*, not the hating business. Nevertheless there are seven specific things God's Word tells us He hates (Proverbs 6:17-19):

A proud look
A lying tongue
Hands that shed innocent blood
A heart that devises wickedness
Feet that are swift in running to mischief
A false witness that speaks lies
He that sows discord among the brethren

Where we recognize ourselves as fitting into any of these categories, it's time to go fox hunting—to kill the spoilers. Whatever the spoiler, we can seek and find release from its clutches through a forgiving spirit.

11

But I Can't Forgive Myself

*We prejudice our case when we fail to call in
the only One who can intercede for us.*

AT THE CLOSE of a luncheon I had spoken at, I was
making my way to the book table when I felt a little tug on
my sleeve. A teary-eyed young woman then said, "I heard
what you were saying about forgiving ourselves, but I just
can't do it," and the tears spilled over.

Noting her name tag I asked, "Would you like to talk
about it, Susan?" and we edged away from the stream of
women. In a quiet corner she poured out her tragic story.
She had lost her four-month-old baby daughter through
crib death. *"And it was all my fault,"* she moaned. "I should
never have left her alone in her crib. I'll *never* be able to
forgive myself."

Peggy's dad laments, "I let my daughter take the car out.
I knew the streets were icy. I'll never forgive myself for
that. It's my fault she got in that accident. And now look at
her, helpless — in a wheelchair. Oh, I'll *never* forgive
myself."

Grandma Andrews stands over a child's hospital bed. She wipes her eyes as she says piteously, "It's all your grandma's fault, Billy." Then half aloud she adds, "How could I have been so careless? John and Alice trusted me to look after Billy. But I just turned my head and there he was out on the street." She covered her eyes with her hands as though to blot out the sight of a motorcycle that roared onto their block and struck down her three-year-old grandson.

"How can I ever *forgive myself?*" she moaned.

Sandra put the receiver back on the hook, a stricken look on her face. "Oh, *no.*" She was almost screaming. "A heart attack. Now I'll never be able to tell Mom how much I loved her. Oh, why didn't I go home last weekend? I knew she was sick and I wouldn't give up my own plans to go see her. I'll never forgive myself for that. Oh, *Mom—*"

"I sent my husband to his grave unhappy," a widow, Jane, regrets. "One thing he always wanted was a set of power tools, and I talked him out of it. Now he's gone. I can't forgive myself for being so mean in depriving him of what would have given him such pleasure in his retirement."

Grief combined with remorse that won't quit, adding up to an intolerable burden of guilt.

Why does guilt take such hold? Why is it so difficult to rid oneself of guilt feelings?

There are a number of reasons.

Since, by heritage and upbringing we are all different personalities, our ability to forgive ourselves may also differ. Nevertheless, there are certain factors that apply to most people.

One is the *inability to forget.*

Somehow, when a person feels he has been the cause (even unwittingly) of harm coming to someone else, it's difficult to erase the memory. It keeps coming up, so the guilt feelings are reinforced.

Two: *the need for punishment.*

The person who is burdened with remorse over some deed feels he deserves to be punished. Since the people around him—understanding that what he did was not

100

intentional — are not going to judge and fix blame on him, he punishes himself by feeling relentless guilt. He fixes the blame on himself.

Three: *The guilt feelings may (subconsciously) be preferable,* more tolerable than the remorse, the "Oh, *if only I had* — " that's eating at the very heart of the individual.

Four: *Inability to emotionally accept that God forgives* and forgives and forgives. It's one thing to believe with the head that God forgives all our iniquities; that He is slow to anger and abounding in lovingkindness (see Psalm 103:3,8). It's quite another thing to relay that message to the heart, to internalize it to the point of *feeling forgiven.*

Five: *A distorted sense of humility.*

There are people who seem to feel, Who am I that God should forgive this awful thing I've done? And no amount of assurance from God Himself through His Word can change their attitude. Feeling unworthy of being forgiven, they cannot emotionally translate God's promises into their own situation and let the Holy Spirit resolve the guilt question.

Six: *A lack of demonstrated forgiveness.*

Others carry around a load of guilt as though it were luggage and they were always on a journey (a guilt trip). Nothing in their background or experience has either equipped or prepared them to accept forgiveness. Dan, a man in his late 30's diagnosed his own problem. "My dad never forgave me. As a kid, no matter what I did wrong, it was always added to everything my dad could dig up from my past. Even little faults, he never forgave them. So I've grown up suspecting anybody who said to me, 'I forgive you.' And I certainly have a hard time ever forgiving myself."

Psychologists generally agree that a child views God in heaven as he views his own father. Therefore when the father is harsh, judgmental, non-forgiving, the child grows up with all these negative concepts, and they are hard to change.

Is there no hope for such people?

Yes, there is, both hope and help.

It will not be a giant leap but a series of steps; these steps will vary with the individual.

Taking an Objective Look

One necessary step is to consider carefully the circumstances that spawned the guilt feelings with which you are now having difficulty. This will take time, for at first it's hard to be objective, to come to the place where you realize "it wasn't my fault." When you can get rid of the blame you've heaped on yourself, healing can begin.

Susan, who lost her baby through crib death, *can* come to see that she could not have prevented the tragedy. The medical profession is at a loss to explain this mysterious disease that claims babies without warning. Gradually, Susan can come to terms with what happened. Ultimately, while it will not bring back her baby, she will be able to live with herself and forgive herself.

Generally we arrive at this level of trust through personal communication with the Lord, rather than through "Job's comforters" who tend to have all the answers as to why disaster strikes us.

Don't Pile on More

One of the hindrances to feeling free from guilt over a specific happening is the tendency to add this one thing to a pile of others. It then takes on huge proportions. Take the woman whose husband died without ever knowing the pleasure of handling his own set of power tools. Undoubtedly, as she continues to dwell on this, other things came to mind: "I should have (done this and that)," and the shoulds or should nots gnaw like a rat at her peace of mind. She views herself as a totally "bad wife." If she were to isolate the thing that haunts her — the tools — from their entire life together which may have been quite happy, she might be able to see the one thing in its true perspective. A man *can* live and be reasonably happy *without* power tools. She needs to tell herself, "I in no way contributed to my husband's death by discouraging him from buying these tools."

She need not go throughout the rest of her life feeling

"I can't forgive myself." It's difficult, however, for logic to take over while emotions are running high. Hopefully, one day she will be able to see the relative unimportance of what is plaguing her — and begin to know the release of feeling forgiven.

When God Forgives

The essence of feeling and knowing forgiveness through appropriating what God has provided, is that we enjoy peace of heart, mind and emotions. We can then move on to be productive for Him as examples of His grace.

No one who ever lived has *not* needed God's forgiveness.

And those who have accepted forgiveness have much to share and contribute.

Take Peter. Peter, who bragged, "Even though all may fall away because of You, I will never fall away" (Matthew 26:33), then turned coward and denied His Lord! We read that he wept bitterly afterward (Matthew 26:75). Suppose he had slumped into a lifetime I-can't-forgive-myself slough of despondency! What if, even after the risen Christ had met with him and forgiven him, even after Peter had been publicly acknowledged and commissioned by the Lord on the shores of Galilee in the presence of the other disciples, he had not been able to feel truly forgiven?

Peter never forgot his deplorable conduct. Yet it's he who gives us the beautiful assurance of what we are worth in the sight of God: "You were not redeemed with perishable things like silver or gold...but with precious blood...the blood of Christ" (1 Peter 1:18,19). And if "redeemed" says anything, it is that we were found on a scrap heap where a "redeemer" gave us back our worth. Peter didn't let the former things prevent him from being a follower of Christ *to the death.*

And what of Paul, the persecutor?

Of all people, the Apostle Paul might have dragged his way through life lamenting, "I'll never forgive myself. I can't sleep at night for my part in the death of Stephen — and oh, the pain I inflicted upon so many other believers!"

Such self-recrimination could have kept Paul bound in chains of futile remorse to the end of his days following his life-changing encounter with the resurrected Christ on the road to Damascus. Paul did not let that happen. Not that he ever forgot his pre-conversion behavior, nor did he ever minimize the enormity of it. "...I used to persecute the church of God beyond measure" (Galatians 1:13); and again in 1 Timothy 1:13, he refers to himself as being before a blasphemer, a persecutor and injurious: the "chief of sinners" he called himself.

Whatever our pre-conversion state of behavior, you and I can learn much from Paul's balanced attitude. Somehow he recognized early that lifelong, abject remorse on his part would serve neither God nor man. He accepted the exceeding and abundant grace of our Lord (1 Timothy 1:14) and appropriated God's forgiveness. The Lord of the harvest had a plan for this zealous man, and it must not be blighted through futile regrets. (I don't think Paul had a classic evangelistic sermon on "From Persecutor to Persecuted" to draw attention to his old life.) He had apparently come to terms with his own guilt and God's limitless forgiveness toward him. He understood his mission, that he would be (v. 16) a pattern to others who would believe, showing forth the long-suffering of Christ. Paul must have been a great encouragement to those who might have been in doubt as to how far the love of Christ would extend itself on their behalf. He would offer hope to all such people.

The Christian who asserts, "I can never forgive myself," is a poor example of the one he professes to love the trust. "But who would take *me* for an example?" this person might counter. It's good for us to keep in mind that no matter how weak our faith may be, if we call ourselves Christian, we can be sure that *someone* is watching and being influenced; perhaps they are viewing you or me as the only Christian they know—and judging all Christians accordingly. So, for the sake of others as well as ourselves, we should take a firm grasp of God's forgiveness:

For the love of God is broader

Than the measure of man's mind;
And the heart of the Eternal
Is most wonderfully kind.*

Acknowledging Our Limits

Psychologist Maurice E. Wagner tells his clients, "Don't hold yourself responsible for what you cannot control."

How comforting for the grandmother who saw her little grandson run down by the motorcycle, if she would latch on to this concept. We *are* responsible only for what it's in our power to do something about. Yet how many go around year after year blaming themselves, unable to forgive themselves for what was beyond their control.

Wagner adds, "We have a primary responsibility to God to forgive ourselves. The person who does not forgive someone whom God has forgiven (himself or herself) is taking a prerogative over God Himself."

If we "can't forgive ourselves," we are refuting the truth of Romans 5:1 and 8:1:

Therefore being justified by faith, we have peace with God through our Lord Jesus Christ.

There is therefore now no condemnation to those who are in Christ Jesus.

We Can't Change God's Mind

"I don't see how you can forgive yourself, Michael. I know *I* can't," said Arlene. Their teenage son had just been picked up by the police for peddling dope. The mother's emotions could not be denied, but there was a certain smugness in her attitude.

Hanging on to guilt — as though ours is a special case — makes no difference to God. He does not have to stretch His principles to provide forgiveness.

Sandra, the girl whose mother died without the assurance of her daughter's love, can go on feeling guilty.

*From the hymn, "There's a Wideness in God's Mercy" *Great Hymns of the Faith,* p. 444. Singspiration (Zondervan Publishing House) © 1968.

Or, she can appropriate *God's* love and His all-encompassing forgiveness and go on to help other young people who need the lesson she has learned the hard way.

It's not how big or how little, how common or how unique the sin we commit; it's not how many times we sin and come short of God's mark. None of these. God forgives us on grounds of Christ's atoning death.

And God is not going to change His mind.

It Takes More Than Head Knowledge

"*Don't keep preaching to me that God forgives.* I'm tired of hearing that," Phyllis said. "Tell me how I can *feel* it, then maybe I can forgive myself for all the things I've done wrong."

Pauline had the same problem and she told me how she overcame it.

"I used to envy the people I knew who seemed so secure in their faith. Oh, they would slip as we all do, but they knew what to do to get back into a good relationship with God. Me? I could never forgive myself, and one day I realized I had never actually *felt* God's forgiveness."

"What made the change? How *did* you manage to feel it and then to forgive yourself?" I asked, very much intrigued.

"I'm afraid it's going to sound oversimplified," she answered, "but oh, it was so real and wonderful! I remember so well. One day I just couldn't stand it any longer, the way I felt. So I prayed, 'Lord, I can't *feel forgiven.* But Your Word tells me that You do forgive, and so I believe You.' I found myself saying out loud, 'By faith I *choose* to believe You and trust You will help me with *feeling* forgiven in Your timing' — and *then* the feeling came. Ever since that day I've had no problem with forgiving myself."

Pauline had experienced what Henry Ward Beecher must have meant when he said,*

God pardons like a mother who kisses the offense into everlasting forgetfulness.

*Forty Thousand Quotations, p. 759, © Christian Herald 1914.

106

Some people have other areas of difficulty in accepting God's forgiveness.

A few days ago I received this little note from a woman I'll call Joanne:

> Jeanette,
>
> I hope your book on *forgiveness* includes a chapter on forgiving *oneself*.
>
> Probably the most difficult thing in my spiritual life is accepting forgiveness of the sin I've committed *since I received the Lord as my Savior*. I don't know how to handle that.

Someone needs to help Joanne realize that there is no time limit clause in the forgiveness God so freely offers. "If we confess our sins, He is faithful and righteous to forgive us our sins and to cleanse [keep on cleansing] us from all unrighteousness" (1 John 1:9).

The Lord's Prayer is a give-us-*this-day* prayer; it was Jesus Himself who taught us to ask for forgiveness "when you pray"; whatever the time. That certainly includes post-salvation forgiveness.

Making the Right Approach

Have you sometimes shaken your head in frustration at the run-around you get when trying to approach some bureaucratic official?

God is not like that.

"One door and only one," an old Gospel chorus goes, speaking of our approach to God. And Jesus said, "I am the door . . ." (John 10:9). We must "draw near to God through Him, since He always lives to make intercession for them" (Hebrews 7:25). To approach a Holy God without the one intercessor He has provided would be tantamount to insisting on being your own defense attorney in a suit you could only lose by doing so. With Christ at our side, no argument against us can stand. We will emerge from the courtroom gloriously exonerated, free from guilt—and *feeling* forgiven. We can then forgive ourselves.

There is not one reasonable argument for not forgiving
oneself!

To err—
Oh, that I know
But to forgive?
That I would learn from You
Who have so loved that You forgave
The worse that sinful man could do.
Teach me, that I
Not only will forgive
The one who's caused me hurt or senseless pain
But that I'll grant *myself* forgiveness
Just as You
Have cleansed, absolved, forgiven even me.
This *is* forgiveness
Full and free
To *feel* forgiven—by Thee.*

**From *Tomorrow's At My Door,* by Jeanette Lockerbie. Fleming H.
Revell, © 1973.

12
Forget the Numbers

Keeping score says, "I didn't forgive you."

"**WHY DO YOU** keep asking me to forgive you?" Cynthia's grandmother said rather irritably. "Haven't I forgiven you enough times already?" And Cynthia, with the sometimes clear-eyed insight of a child, said as she turned rather sadly away, "Grandma doesn't really forgive me; she just says she does."

Grandmas and parents were not the first to infer that forgiveness should have a quota.

Never noted for patience, Peter turned to the Lord one day and asked, "How many times must I forgive my brother?" then proceeded to answer his own question with "seven times?"

Peter had a precedent for thinking in sevens. Luke recounts the instance when Jesus said: "If your brother sins, rebuke him; and if he repents, forgive him. And if he sins against you seven times a day, and returns to you seven times, saying 'I repent,' forgive him" (Luke 17:3,4).

Perhaps Peter was only half listening. He heard the seven, but not the seven in one day. Now, in response to his question, "How many times?" the Lord says not seven but *seventy times seven* (Matthew 18:21, 22).

109

Can you see the big fisherman doing some quick calculation?

This is not the only instance in the New Testament where the Lord Jesus used hyperbole to drive home a great principle. (See "the alms and the trumpets"—Matthew 6:2.) But what if Peter had taken the words literally!

Jesus had used a specific figure in His directive concerning forgiveness. Four hundred and ninety times, He had said. Had Jesus been speaking literally, and had Peter so understood it, Peter and all who later believed in Jesus and sought to obey Him would have been bound by the "490 times."

Think what that would have meant. We would have to become "forgiveness accountants." This would entail the use of scorecards or a notebook for keeping strict accounts; for making sure we forgave *not one time more* than we should. The process could become quite involved as we find it necessary to forgive more and more people more and more times. We would need a sheaf of pages, one for each potential trespasser against us.

At meetings, to demonstrate this absurdity, I use a chalkboard or a large sheet of paper marked with squares. I check off the first square. *There, I've forgiven that person once. She has all these chances left.* So when this same person does another thing that calls for my forgiving her, I find her chart with the one check mark. I raise my chalk or pen to check square number two, but—I'm stopped! Something inside won't let me make that other mark. Why? Because the first one is there accusing me, "You didn't forgive the first time."

A silly practice? Then what was our Lord really teaching Peter—and you and me—by His hyperbole, His 490 times?

"We don't keep score, Peter," is the essence of His teaching. "We forgive and forgive and forgive *as often as the other repents,* times without number."

Why We Keep Score

We don't generally stop and analyze why we do every

little thing. But we do need to ask, "Why am I unwilling to forgive John or Mary or whoever?"

Sharon's mother didn't care who heard her say, "I'll never again forgive my daughter. I've forgiven her once too often already." In this mother's book her daughter had used up her forgiveness quota. The mother's intent was to hurt her daughter as she felt the daughter had hurt her — to pay her back.

It's a fallacy, however, that a person is always hurt just because someone withholds forgiveness. In many instances the other person is totally unaware of the negative or vengeful feelings held against him. The unforgiving person is the one who really suffers, because an unforgiving spirit leads to guilt and its bad effects on the body, mind and spirit.

Another reason is that we might justify ourselves.

Elisabeth argued with herself, "If I forgive Laura for what she did to me — sneaking behind my back and getting the job I should have gotten — then I'm saying she was *right* in what she did. I could never let her have that satisfaction. I might forgive her for some things, but not that." As though to bolster her shaky argument, she pulled herself up straight, arched her neck defiantly, and added, "and *I know that she was wrong.*" Such thinking justified Elizabeth in her own eyes, however contrary it might be to what she knew the Bible had to say.

Some people continue to hold a grudge, to keep score, all because they have allowed one bad experience to color their whole thinking on the subject.

Eighteen-year-old Doreen stormed into the house and spouted, "Don't expect me to try *that* again!"

"Try what?" her mother asked.

"You kow. I told you I was going over to cousin Jean's to ask her to forgive me about that disagreement we had last month. Well, I said a lot of things I shouldn't have. She did too, for that matter. But I know what the Bible says we should do, so I prayed, Mom." She appealed for understanding and continued, "Then I went and asked Jean to forgive me. And what do you think she *said?*"

"What?"

Hands on her hips and head in the air, Doreen portrayed her cousin's answer, "'*Forgive* you? Whatever for? What do *I* care about whether you're sorry or not, it doesn't make one bit of difference, it's not that important to me!' Can you *believe* it, Mom? She humiliated me; she discounted my *feelings,* and I was just trying to do the right thing. Now I'll never forgive her; and it'll be a long time before I try that again. I'll think twice before going to ask anybody to forgive me. I tell you, Mom, *it just doesn't work!*"

Doreen's reaction is understandable. Nevertheless, the other person's attitude and response does not lessen our responsibility, doesn't negate God's directive to us to be forgiving. The Bible does not qualify itself with "If this," or "If that." Such an experience as Doreen's does, however, explain why she and others who have received such a response would hesitate to risk a repeat performance. Rather, they continue to justify themselves for not being forgiving, and they nurture the weeds of unforgiveness and guilt.

As we discussed in chapter nine, people "keep score" because they, themselves, never knew real forgiveness as they were growing up. Never having felt forgiven, they are still getting even.

What a delight it was to me, then, to have a bright young woman come up and talk with me after a meeting. I can still see her eager face as she said, "I'm going back to square one and blot it out; no more keeping score for me."

The Importance of Perspective

Sometimes we attribute more importance to an incident than it is worth. For a trifling offense we will "punish" someone for years. At the same time we rob ourselves of the joy that comes from exercising forgiveness.

Anna heard that her brother and his family would possibly be passing through her town on their way to a convention. She immediately baked and cooked and shined up the house. By mid-afternoon she was tired and irritable. When evening came and the company had not arrived, she was furious at them and took it out on her own family. Then, for years she would have nothing to do with her brother and his family.

"How could they treat me so?" she complained.

If she had taken a few minutes to think it over, all that had happened was that she was briefly disappointed that the folks had not stopped for coffee and a bite to eat and a short visit. That was the most she could have expected at the time. Seeing the incident for what it was—not what she had built it up to be in her own mind—she could have made light of it. Her own family could then have happily enjoyed the treats she had baked (and it hadn't hurt the house to have a good cleaning!).

Anna could take a leaf from the book of Amy Carmichael's life. The famed missionary to India came to the place where she considered every slight, every word of criticism, every irritation and every trial that came her way, in the light of eternity. A recurrent theme in her writings is, "Since it is not going to matter in eternity, why should I let it affect me *now?*"

When we have eyes only for the hurts of the *now*, we blind ourselves to the good and happy things that are going on in our lives. So it is important that we keep the daily slights in their true perspective, and be willing to keep the forgiveness channels open.

If We Got What We Deserve

One day I watched as a boy pleaded with his father to stop thrashing a younger brother.

"Be quiet and mind your own business," the father snapped, as he applied his belt once more with all his force behind it.

I couldn't know nor was it my business to inquire as to what had occasioned the father's anger and his severe punishing of his boy. All I know is what I saw and heard. At one point the man screamed, "You're just getting what you deserve. I've given you plenty of chances. I've always forgiven you—but *no more.*"

What if God were to keep score?

How many "chances" would we get for lying, for cheating, for hating someone, for being a tale-bearer, for jealousy, for criticism. And what of the short-comings and the "sins of omission"? How long would our quota last? How long would it be before the well of forgiveness had run dry and all our sins from that point on were held against us?

But God is not like that.

We dole out "what they deserve"; God, for Christ's sake, gives us what we do not deserve or merit: *limitless* forgiveness.

I wonder if the father who had shut off forgiveness toward his own son ever ponders his own standing before God! Would he, I wonder, really like to get what *he* deserves, all the time? Since it's a proven fact that children almost always view God as they view their own father, what a distorted image of God that badly-beaten young boy must have of God in heaven. And how hard it will be for someone to reach through to him with the assurance that God's attitudes are not those of his earthly father.

Too Good to Be True

Sally had come to know the Lord through a neighborhood Bible study group. She appeared to understand and to be grasping the teaching; she seemed happy in her new-found faith. But after about two months she appeared one morning at the Bible teacher, Mabel's, home and said, "Here, I'm giving you back the nice Bible you gave me." Invited into the living room, Sally kept on talking: "This Christian life is too high-level for me; I try, but I keep falling back into my old ways. I keep asking God to forgive me, again and again. Now, before I exhaust His patience and He gives up on me, *I'm* giving up." And she placed the nearly new Bible on the coffee table.

Mabel let her talk out what was on her heart, then took her hand and said gently, "Sally, *God will never* give up on you, you can be sure of that."

"But you don't know...."

Mabel picked up the Bible and leafed to Psalm 103:

114

"Look at this," she said and pointed to the tenth verse. "Read for yourself." Sally read aloud, "He has not dealt with us according to our sins, nor rewarded us according to our iniquities." She looked thoughtful then exclaimed, "That's just what you said, that God doesn't give up on people like me. It's too good to be true!" After more discussion of the God who is abounding in mercy, Sally left with a new look on her face, a new spring in her step, a greater understanding of the God who doesn't keep score, and with her *Bible* in her hand!

A Heaped-up Store of Forgiveness

Not always is it the number of times God forgives that has the most meaning; it can be *the magnitude of one time!*

Josh, a man in his eighties, a guide and trapper in Northern Canada, had never darkened a church door in his life. Moreover, he had cruelly kept his wife and sons from ever attending church or Sunday school.

A new young preacher came to their outlying town, and daring the wrath of "Old Josh" (who had been known to kick more than one preacher out of his home), went visiting. Because Josh found that he and the new preacher had a common interest in history, he permitted the visits to continue. As long as the conversation centered around heroes such as the Duke of Wellington, the old man was alert and participated. But when the Bible was opened he would mutter, "can't hear a thing," or he would angrily reach for his cane and hobble out of the house.

This went on for about a year, then a bad fall confined Josh to his bed. One day, hearing voices in the kitchen, he called out, "If that's the preacher, *send him in.*" Then the old man wasted no time. "Preacher," he began, "I've been lying to you all the time. I've *heard* all right. Now I'm asking you, is it *true* what you've been reading to Maggie (his wife)? Is it *really true* that God forgives sinners?"

Again the preacher assured him from the Word of God, but Josh interrupted, "But would that include *me*, preacher?"

It took time and the repetition of, "Though your sins are

as scarlet, they will be white as snow..." (Isaiah 1:18), and Hebrews 7:25, "He is able to save forever those who draw near to God through Him, since He always lives to make intercession for them." As a light of understanding began to break over his weatherbeaten face, Josh said, "Well, preacher, if all you tell me is true—if He *is* that kind of God—call Maggie, for I can never look into the face of God and ask Him to forgive me, until I ask my wife to forgive me for the awful way I've treated her." The incredulous wife, who had prayed most of her life for this moment, had no problem in forgiving her husband. Then Josh lifted his eyes heavenward and prayed, "God, have mercy on this old reprobate and save me for Jesus' sake."

God heard that plea. It was as though, in addition to His own unfailing grace, He had counted the more than 70 x 7 times a loving, long-suffering Christian wife had forgiven her abusive, unloving husband. It was one of those once-in-a-pastor's-lifetime conversions. (I know it's true, for the pastor was my late husband, the Rev. E. A. Lockerbie.) Josh miraculously changed. Like the woman in the Gospels who, having been forgiven much, loved much, he lived out the rest of his days never missing a chance to tell of the God who can save even "an old reprobate like me." His sons, their children, and others in the community were so impressed and convinced that many of them followed his example and turned to the Lord.

When Silence Is Not Golden

Many a person has grown up with unhappy memories of a parent who demonstrated an unforgiving spirit by frozen silence.

"My mother is a Christian, my dad is not," Jon told me, "and our home was often a very unhappy place. Whenever Mom was mad at Dad, *which was often,* she wouldn't speak to him. Sometimes it went on for days. Dad would try to make up, but Mom just sat there, stony faced and tight-lipped. Nothing could have been more uncomfortable than our home at such times. I hated to go home. It was hard to believe then that Christianity was a good thing for people, with my mother's behavior as our example. She was never able to persuade my dad to accept the Lord. I used to think, *If she would only forgive him and show him some love.* Instead, she alternately preached at him and gave him the silent treatment."

What if Jon's mother had been like Maggie!

It's hard to be the victim of another's aggression, or non-cooperation, or whatever brings us frustration or grief. Jesus knows all about that. He suffered every indignity, all the misunderstandings, all the vengeance and hatred humanity could vent upon Him. He "took it" even unto death. He forgave. He keeps on forgiving and forgiving and forgiving, forgetting about "How many times should I forgive?"

By His Spirit, He will enable you and me to forgive 490 times, and more.

13

The High Cost of Not Forgiving

The price is never "right."

WHAT IS IT worth? we ask. What is it going to cost me? Everything in life has its price.

Sam, an avowed atheist boasts, "I never asked forgiveness of either God or man. And I don't go around forgiving other people who ask *me*. Guess I'll carry that stuff to my grave."

"You'll carry it *beyond* the grave, my friend," warned a concerned Christian.

The Lord Jesus, who knew more about forgiving than anyone else who ever walked this earth, taught that if we will not forgive others, we will forfeit God's forgiveness. So the ultimate cost is *eternal*.

But what of the cost here and now? How does an unforgiving spirit affect various aspects of our life and witness?

The Health Factor

Lillian had seen her medical doctor for what she described to him as "vague pains." Examination, a work-up, and continued attention from her doctor didn't help. She still complained of "not feeling good."

Sessions with a psychologist likewise did little to rid her of her pains. Finally, in near desperation, for she was a woman accustomed to enjoying excellent health, she went to her minister. An understanding and godly man, he listened attentively to her "symptoms." "And nothing I've tried has helped one little bit," she concluded.

Aware that she had already sought both medical and psychological counsel and help, he was silent for a few minutes. Then, with a concerned expression on his face and in his voice, he suggested, "Could it be that you might possibly have a problem over someone you need to forgive?"

She hung her head, and he had to bend closer to hear, "I haven't wanted to think it might be that, but — yes, Pastor, I do have such a problem." She went on to tell of her resentment and animosity toward another member of her family. "It's almost a year since it happened, but it's never out of my mind for long."

"Well, now I'm no doctor, Lillian," he responded, "but I can offer you a prescription. Holding a grudge is something none of us can afford for long. The price is too high."

"Oh, I *know*," she agreed.

"You know your Bible. I don't have to tell you all that God says to us about forgiveness. But just let's look at this verse," the minister urged and he turned to Ephesians 4:32, "Be kind one to another, tender-hearted, forgiving each other, just as God in Christ also has forgiven you."

"I'm going to *do* it, Pastor," Lillian assured him. "It will be hard, but with the Lord's help I'm going to obey His Word. I will forgive her — and oh, I feel better already. Thank you for being honest with me." Then, as she reached the door she turned around and with a smile said, "And don't you be saying you're no doctor!"

Ingrid Bergman made a helpful comment along the line of forgiveness as it affects one's health:

Good health is having a poor memory for the bad

things people have done to you.*

The Cost to the Church

How many churches struggle with maintaining a credible image in their community, while just a very few in an otherwise consistent membership mar that image.

"Hey, Steve," a fellow team member said, "How about coming to church with me next week? We've having one of your favorite players talk to us. And anyway it wouldn't hurt you to start going to church," he grinned.

"Don't try that line on me," Steve said defensively. "I know a whole lot of church people. I've seen how they treat each other, holding grudges and all. Church people don't forgive one another. Sorry, but no thanks, pal."

We can't know where Steve acquired his concepts and impressions of Christians. He lumps all "church people" together and judges us all by the ones he cannot admire. Whatever his justification, this blocked the efforts of another Christian to interest Steve in a Gospel meeting.

Christians need to be believable. The non-Christian has his standards, his expectations of those who profess to follow Christ (normally, he doesn't have the same expectations of himself; he knows he can't attain such a level on his own!). When he sees the believer as "no better than I am," it stretches his credibility and makes a skeptic of him. It's disastrous to the cause of Christ when people see us being unloving. We are exhorted not to "bite and devour one another" (Galatians 5:15). We won't if we cultivate a spirit of forgiveness.

Sometimes the church pays a high price in *unanswered prayer.*

A suburban church was praying fervently as they looked forward to a scheduled series of meetings with a Bible teacher whose ministry God was blessing. Congregational interest was high in all departments but the high school. A kind of apathy had settled upon this group; nothing spiritual had been happening for some time.

Following a prayer meeting called the week prior to the

*From a Dick Cavett interview.

121

special meetings, one of the young people, Mildred, asked the pastor if she might speak with him. She had not gone far before her voice broke and the tears started to flow. Between sobs she stammered, "Pastor—it's me. I'm the one who will be holding up the blessing when the meetings begin. I'm keeping God from answering all that prayer I heard tonight."

"Tell me about it, Mildred," her pastor urged gently.

"Oh, Pastor. It's Peggy and me. We had a falling out over something I said about her in fun one day. I tried to apologize and to make it up to her but..." She bit her lip, then continued, "It was all my fault. And I want to do something so we will have good results at our meetings. I don't want to miss all the blessing either. But what can I *do?*" she appealed. "Peggy won't speak to me."

The pastor let her talk out all that was in her heart, then he prayed with her and suggested, "Come over to the parsonage tomorrow evening—7 or so. I just may have an idea."

Mildred arrived on time and the pastor's wife ushered her into the living room. There, with the pastor, stood Peggy. She stiffened when she saw Mildred. There was an awkward moment, then Mildred took some quick steps to cross the room toward Peggy. "Please forgive me, Peg. I want us to be friends again. I've missed you."

Peggy's response was lost in the girls' tearful reunion. A joyous time followed as the pastor and his wife rejoiced with their young church members. Then, repentant, forgiven, restored to each other, cleansed of all that had kept them apart, they more than made up for the time they had lost. And the church never had such answers to their prayers! All because one member would not let herself be a hindrance to the working of the Holy Spirit in the group. She chose rather to forgive.

The Family Pays a High Price

Children learn most of their attitudes at home. Little sister breaks her brother's favorite toy. He screams, small boy style, "I'll *never forgive you!*" So next time she might be the victim; her favorite doll comes to grief. How does she react? Exactly as her brother did. More than likely they didn't have a good model in either parent.

The world-renowned violinist, Isaac Stern, will not play in former Nazi countries. The memories of atrocities are still too raw. Questioned about this policy, he stated in a talk program on television, "Though I myself will not play for these people, it's my hope that my grandchildren will play for their grandchildren. It's not my desire or intention to leave a legacy of hate to my children."

Nevertheless, what we are, what we do rubs off on our families much more than our words of good intention.

Jimmie, a nine-year-old, often brags, "I'm just like my dad. He never says he's sorry. Not for *anything*. And he never says, 'Forgive me,' to anybody, either."

Predictably, unless he changes, young Jimmie is heading for a life of alienating almost everybody with whom he comes in contact. He'll pay a high price for being "like his dad" in this respect.

Deliberately choosing not to forgive, as a way of life, is rank disobedience to the revealed will of God, to the Word of God. Such disobedience will exact its own toll. It does not generally stop with one generation, either.

The Cost in Productivity

Our minds are constantly absorbed with one thought or another. The Bible makes that so clear and tells us the end result, "As a man thinks in his heart, so is he" (Proverbs 23:7). So *is* he—present tense. We are what we are thinking at the moment.

What are the ramifications of this fact? Does it not mean that if we dwell on negative things for long periods of time we will act negatively. So the one who will not forgive but who keeps nurturing thoughts of how someone has mistreated him (whether true or not), can't give his mind and heart to more productive activity.

I can personally attest to that. A number of years ago, I occupied my mind with thoughts of how badly I had been treated in a certain situation. I felt quite justified in my own mind for not forgiving the people concerned. Then one day it came to me that I was having a dearth of ideas for my writing. The creative juices were not flowing as formerly. Why? Bitterness, self-pity and resentment were clogging the stream of creativity. But the Holy Spirit was too faithful to let me remain in that "far country" of the soul. He convicted me and pricked my conscience. He reminded me of *how much* the Lord Jesus Christ had forgiven me, the high cost He had paid that I might have release from negative feelings (if I would appropriate His grace).

I got the message. I took the scriptural steps and in a once-and-for-all commitment of the situation to God, I was enabled to overcome the feelings that had engulfed me and made my days almost totally unproductive.

Well might we heed and obey Paul's counsel concerning the control of our thought life, when he wrote (Philippians 4:8):

Whatever is true...honorable...right...pure...lovely...of good repute; if there is any excellence and if anything worthy of praise, let your mind dwell on these things.

Not a negative thought among them! And the inferences would seem to be that when our minds and hearts are filled with these thoughts, there's no room for detrimental, unproductive thinking.

To be sure, there are instances when we hear of a person, "The only thing that kept him going (after some bitter experience) was his hatred; it just drove him." This can happen. But ultimately the person will be driven to emotional disaster. Hatred and bitterness are poison to the human heart and mind. They finally cost more than one can afford to pay.

The Cost to One's Pride

"*I'm* not going to humble myself and go and say I'm sorry," Phyllis told her husband. "Why should I? and anyway, if I do, I'll never hear the end of it."

This can be true. There *are* people who gloat over the one who comes seeking forgiveness from them, who never lets the person forget, in the manner of one who still owes a debt.

But there are rewards, as well as a cost to one's pride, for the Christian who will humble himself is on good firm ground with the Lord.

God is able to deal with the person who does not graciously respond when someone says "Please forgive me." And meanwhile, He blesses the one who is willing to humble himself. His Word tells us, "For everyone who exalts himself shall be humbled, and he who humbles himself shall be exalted" (Luke 14:11).

Then there are the "honest" kind, like Carla.

"I'm not a forgiving person," she admits quite freely. "But neither do I pretend to be. I'm *honest,*" she justifies herself. And her pride in being honest makes her stumble over the fact that she could be both honest and forgiving; the one does not exclude the other.

There's a high price to pay when pride prevents us from exhibiting a spirit of forgiveness.

When We Pay the Price

Every time Clara and her friend Pauline met, the same subject came up: Clara reiterating what another woman had done to her.

"If I could only forget!" she would sigh, then go on to relate all the details of the injury she had suffered at the other person's hands.

Pauline had no desire to hear the oft-repeated tale but she cared for her friend and didn't want to add to her problems by appearing unsympathetic. But she knew that Clara needed to handle her feelings some other way, for her own well-being.

Pauline prayed about it quite a bit, and the next time she and Clara met and the same subject came up, Pauline asked, "Do you really want to forget, Clara?"

"Oh, yes, but I know I never can," Clara answered.

"I think you might be able to. Let me tell you about

125

something my pastor said the other day." A spark of interest came into Clara's eyes and she looked expectantly at Pauline.

"Here is what he said that so impressed me," Pauline continued, "'I am convinced that we can do almost anything, if we *pray* about it and *plan,* and *make up our mind* to do it.'"

Clara was silent for a moment then she said thoughtfully, "I *have* prayed about this problem — maybe not enough, though. But I can't say I ever *planned* to do something about it. And I have to admit I never have *made up my mind* to resolve it."

"How much does it mean to you to have done with it, Clara," Pauline asked.

"*Plenty,*" said Clara fervently.

The two parted. But Clara could not get what Pauline had said out of her mind. The next morning, leafing through her Bible in search of passages on forgiveness, her eye caught a verse in the psalms, "Thou, Lord, art good, and ready to forgive" (Psalm 86:5).

Am I ready to forgive? She looked into her own heart.

It didn't take too much self-examining in the light of God's Word for Clara to arrive at an answer. *I have not been ready,* she freely admitted to herself. She then got down on her knees and sought help from the God who is always ready to forgive. And the very next day she carried out the plan she had made — to go and humbly seek reconciliation with the other person.

Some days later, Clara and Pauline met for lunch. Immediately, Pauline noticed a new expression on her friend's face. She waited for Clara to explain.

"I tried it — I *tried* it," she exclaimed. "I prayed, planned, and went to make things right. It *worked.* And oh, Pauline, I never felt so good inside in all my life!"

Clara may find it's not all that easy to *forget.* But she will no longer remember with hurt and injury to herself. Whatever happened between another and herself will no longer mar the present for her.

Best of all, it will not shadow her fellowship with Christ, which is too high a price to pay.

For each individual—because we are all different—the cost of harboring and nurturing feelings of unforgiveness may take various forms. But it is an inexorable spiritual law that there *will be* a price—and that price will never be "right."

14
You Can Afford It

*We clog our own emotional machinery when
we refuse to exercise forgiveness.*

THROUGH THE YEARS we have all amassed a store of
forgiveness experiences. They are Christ's favors out-
stretched to you and me, the countless times He has
forgiven us. Why would we not eagerly desire to "pass it
on"?

One woman in the Bible could teach us this lesson. She
dared the scorn and humiliation of the more righteous, to
give, in abandonment, her gratitude for Christ's forgiveness of her sins. She could afford it. Forgiven much, she
loved much and showed it (see Luke 7:36-49). For her
devoted outpouring of the precious contents of her
alabaster box, this woman has been immortalized in
Scripture, as Christ said she would be.

Could we have followed her day-by-day, we would
almost surely have found her to be a consistently forgiving
person, compassionate toward the sinner as she had
experienced Christ's compassion toward her.

But the Bible has another story to tell, the almost
incredible contrast of a man who would not forgive. Found
in Matthew 18:23-25, some versions headline it "The
Parable of the Unmerciful Servant." Briefly, it's the story

of a servant who owed a vast sum to his master but had nothing with which to pay even a portion of it. This debtor was ordered by his master to be sold with all his family so that payment might be made. Then, in response to the servant's pleas and promise to pay, the master was compassionate and forgave the man all of the debt. This forgiven servant, in turn, was owed a small sum by another man. Now would it not follow that having been forgiven so much, this servant would be forgiving? Not so. He violently abused the poor man who could not pay, then cast him into prison.

Both men in this parable Jesus told could afford to forgive. One did; the other refused and was made to suffer just retribution: "In anger his master turned him over to the jailers until he should pay all that he owed" (Matthew 18:34).

Apart from the right or the wrong of it, anyone who has ever extended forgiveness to someone else knows the good feeling that rewards us. We rob ourselves, we clog our own emotional machinery, when we will not forgive.

The Generosity of David

David, "the man after God's own heart" (1 Samuel 13:14; Acts 13:22), knew how to be both giving and forgiving. He knew he could afford it and he showed his forgiveness literally "to the third generation."

One of the most poignant and inspiring stories in all the Old Testament is that concerning David and the grandson of King Saul, a true "Prince and the Pauper" tale. And its happy ending is possibly only because of David's loving, forgiving spirit.

King Saul, out of jealousy and envy, plentifully mixed with malice and resentment, had caused David to become a fugitive from the king's wrath. In caves in the mountains and in the desolate wilderness David took refuge. Yet in all of his problems with King Saul, David did not become bitter. In fact, 1 Samuel 24 relates the dramatic incident of a strategic point at which David could easily have killed Saul (who was hunting David to kill him). David came upon the king, and David's men would have urged him to take revenge, to do away with Saul. If David's act in cutting off a piece of the king's garment was a temporary retaliation, he speedily evidenced his remorse to the king. Ultimately, just before the death of King Saul, David won him over.

But that was not the end of his kind dealings with that family. Both Jonathan and his father, Saul, had pleaded with David not to cut off the line of Saul when they were gone and he was on the throne. David had suffered sufficiently at the hands of Saul that he might be pardoned for not remembering this covenant. But he carried no grudge against the ones who had so harried him for years.

Chapter 9 of 2 Samuel recounts David's diligence to keep his covenant, to the letter. His efforts led to the discovery that one of Jonathan's sons was alive. We could let our imagination roam wildly, but the Bible narrative is itself dramatic. David had just triumphed over the enemies of Israel. His own sons were ruling princes, and his heart must have yearned over his lost friend Jonathan. He inquired, "Is there yet left of the house of Saul that I may show him kindness for Jonathan's sake?" A servant responded, "There is still a son of Jonathan, Mephibosheth," and he added, "He is lame in both feet." (2 Samuel 4:4 explains the circumstances which caused his lameness when he was a child of five.)

There was no gloating on David's part that this was what the house of Saul had come to. Three words were all it took for David to get into action: *"Where is he?"* Surely the next verse is a powerful understatement, "And King David sent and brought him...from Lo-debar." Lo-debar, I have been told, means "the place of poor pasture," surely no source of provision for the grandson of Israel's first king.

The crippled Mephibosheth may at times have talked about his noble birth. Had he been laughed to scorn? "You who are a charity case living off poor servants! Grandson of a king?" Perhaps they laughed behind his back figuring his head was as weak as his feet. But all that was changed in a moment when, in his love and limitless forgiveness, David proved himself a king indeed.

131

The one-time pauper moved into the palace and at the king's bidding, Mephibosheth "ate daily at David's table, as one of the king's sons" (2 Samuel 9:11).

We are not royalty. Few of us will ever, by a grand gesture of demonstrated forgiveness, totally change someone else's station in life. But we can do *something* as we forgive, for when genuine forgiveness is offered and received, everyone concerned profits. Reconciliation benefits parents, children, grandchildren, in-laws, neighbors, the church and the community. And forgiving is something everyone of us can do.

On the personal level, nothing can ensure a conscience-free, good night's sleep, more than the knowledge that as far as we know, there is no unforgiveness in our heart.

Late in 1979 my 96-year-old father went to be with the Lord. For much of his life he had not bothered with anything Christian; ours was not a Bible-reading, praying home. Then, on a memorable night in July 1951, in Brooklyn, New York, my dad gave his heart and life to Jesus Christ. Officiating at the memorial service, my eldest brother, a minister, was able to say, "He was my father; I knew him better than anyone else, and in all my life *I never heard him say anything bad about someone else.*"

I couldn't help but think, *My father left no forgiveness business undone.* Would that the same might be said of all of us when God calls us into His presence.

Keeping a Short Account

The best way to feel reasonably sure we are not piling up forgiveness debts is to deal with each situation as soon as we possibly can.

I was surprised not long ago to receive a little note from a woman I had talked with some days earlier. She was asking me to forgive her. *For what?* was my first thought. I couldn't recall any reason. I read on, and she explained that she had been troubled lest she had used "too strong words" in connection with what we had been talking about. "I may not have been kind," she wrote. "There are many ways of saying things—I am really trying to learn."

I was greatly moved by that note, and I told her so when we again met (within a day or two). Although I really could not relate to her feeling that she had been harsh with her words, or that there was any occasion for me to forgive her, nevertheless I respected the fact that this is how she *did* feel. And it certainly gave me room for thought that she had so speedily sought to correct what to her was unbecoming behavior. Suppose she had let it trouble her without taking the step she did. In her mind the issue would have grown. She couldn't know that I had not felt one bit put out at her words or her tone. Not knowing that, and feeling convicted herself, she might easily have construed any little word or action of mine in a way that could have possibly created misunderstanding between us. She took the better way, the short account route. It's always better to err on the side of an oversensitive conscience than to be deaf to the promptings of the Holy Spirit. It's always advisable to take the scriptural measures for gaining good feelings about ourselves.

I was standing at a crosswalk with a friend, waiting for the traffic light to change. Just as it did and I was stepping off the curb, my friend tugged my arm and said, "Let's not cross here; let's keep on this side."

"OK," I said, wondering a little. Halfway up the next block my friend explained, "Just as the light changed I recognized someone about to cross from the other side. We would have run right into her."

"Would that have been so bad?" I interrupted.

"I just didn't want to meet her. We used to be good friends, until—well, it's a long story, and I don't want to go into it. But she refused to say she was sorry. And I'm not about to be the one to say it."

This unforgiving woman could better afford to be forgiving than to lose friends and have to duck when she sees them coming. In addition she is left without the peace that comes from being right with God and with our fellow men—in this case—*woman.*

Jesus provides this peace for us. It is His legacy: "Peace I leave with you," he assured his sorrowing disciples. But we can refuse it, settling rather for "our rights."

The short account is God's guarantee that we can feel clean. "If we confess our sins, He is faithful and righteous to forgive us our sins and to cleanse us from all unrighteousness" (1 John 1:9). Some Bible scholars interpret it as "keeps on cleansing." Inherent in that version is the recognition of our continual need for cleansing, for forgiveness. It pays, then, to keep a short account with God.

When the Account Gets Out of Hand

Long-held grudges and malice, like undisposed-of garbage, begin to create an undesirable environment.

Unpaid, overdue debts create a host of other problems. So it is when we're not careful about our relationships. God's Word tells us that the only thing we are to owe other people is love: "Owe nothing to anyone except to love one another" (Romans 13:8). We cannot continue to disregard our debts without paying more interest than we can afford.

No one is so poor but that he can always afford to love and forgive; the two cannot be separated.

"We're poor people," an old man once told me, "but one thing we've always managed to do was to keep two bears in our house."

"Two *bears?*" I repeated after him.

With a warm smile he said, "Yes. 'Bear' and 'Forbear'; they are the two bears. And they have kept peace in our midst for many years. In fact, we would never want to be without them in our home."

When we don't bear and forbear, when we fail to be forgiving toward one another, we can become so disgruntled that we make life miserable for those around us. Since, perversely, we tend to save our better behavior for those outside the home, our own dear ones become the target for our unpleasantness.

It's good, then, to look at the whole picture and ask ourselves, Who and how many are suffering daily because of my obstinate, sinful unwillingness to be obedient to God's command to forgive?

Joan, a middle-aged, warm, sensitive woman confided, "I can't seem to do anything right anymore. Michael (her husband) yells at me for nothing. I can't understand it one bit! He's a different man these past few months, not the man I married at all." She went on to pinpoint the time he had begun to change, then reiterated, "I can't seem to do anything right; but I don't know what I'm doing *wrong*."

She was unhappy, and all the more because she was in the dark as to the cause of it.

In this instance, as time proved, the "why" was quite simple. It was rooted in a situation *that did not involve the man's wife* in the least. The husband had lost out on some "good deal" in connection with business colleagues. Disappointed, he had become bitter at these men, blaming them for his misfortune. His bad feelings escalated as he saw another man gain what he had hoped to gain. "I'll never forgive him; I should have won," he kept telling himself. The bitterness turned to hatred that colored his entire outlook, consequently his behavior. His only "friends" were those who would join him in his recriminations. His feelings were all out of proportion to what had caused them, and his wife was the nearest, and safest person he could vent his rage on. He sprayed his hostility all over the place when he was at home. And between dodging the flack and the tongue-lashings, the hapless wife spent her days wondering, *What am I doing wrong?*

Whether or not this home will ever again know peace and harmony depends on the husband's willingness to face up to what *is,* accept what he can't change, and forgive the one against whom he holds the grudge. He may then begin to see what his unkind behavior is doing to his wife. Along the way he will feel the release that comes from forgiving others. It will not bring him the "good deal" he set out to obtain; it will bring him something much more worthwhile, more inwardly satisfying and longlasting.

When, with God's help, we obey and forgive, the Bible offers a beautiful, hope-filled promise: "I will make up to you for the years that the swarming locust has eaten" (Joel 2:25). The locust. Relentless devourer that leaves only devastation in its wake. In nature, God alone can stay the plague of locusts, can reclaim and revitalize the ravished land. Likewise, only God can sweeten and make fruitful a life stultified by a spirit of unforgiveness. And beautifully, those at home, who may have been targets of our bitterness, will then be the beneficiaries of God's good work in effecting change.

And think—we can *afford* to forgive, for in giving forgiveness, the benefits go to everyone.

To Discuss and Act Upon

CHAPTER 1

You've just had a glimpse into the reactions of a number of Christians following a severe trial.

1. What do the attitudes of each reveal about:

   their faith?

   their knowledge of and application of God's Word to their situation?

   How would each have been helped by:
   Ephesians 4:32?
   Hebrews 13:5?
   Hebrews 12:1,2?

2. In the example of Edith and her grudge against her church's minister, her entire relationship with her church was severed.

   Consider:

   How could she have avoided her separation from her church?

   How did her attitude toward the minister affect her attitude toward the entire church?

   What steps might she have taken upon the arrival of a new minister? What, in your opinion, kept Edith from going to him with her problem?

3. In Debbie's case, how did the Lord show her she had indeed forgiven her friend Linda?

4. Do you sometimes find yourself thinking/rationalizing, *but my case is different?* Do you then say, "Lord, you know all things; You know how I've been mistreated. Surely even You can't expect me to forgive and act as if nothing has happened"?

   If such thoughts have occurred to you, how could you deal with them in light of:
   Hebrews 12:1,2?
   Ephesians 4:32?

5. Has the Holy Spirit been nudging you, bringing to mind—perhaps, this very minute—something you need to straighten out? Someone you need to forgive? Someone from whom you need to ask forgiveness?

   You realize that now is the time to heed the promptings of the Holy Spirit within you. But you don't *feel* like doing anything about it. What then?

   Feelings are not to be trusted at such times.

   Think. From what specific situations in your own life have you:

   a. proved God's promises to be with you when you have sought forgiveness and/or been quick to forgive another?

   b. learned to your hurt what happens when you are unwilling to forgive?

6. Two courses are open to you:

   One, you can stifle the voice of the Holy Spirit, telling yourself, "God doesn't mean *me!*"

   Or, two, you can listen and obey.

   Why not pray: "Lord, You know it's going to be hard for me to go and ask for forgiveness. You know I would rather put it off. So, will You please go with me and help me to do *by faith* what Your Spirit is prompting me to do—right now?"

   Then take that first step (literally).

CHAPTER 2

Finding people to listen to us in general is not too easy — everyone seems to want to *talk*. Listening, when a plea for forgiveness is involved, can be crucial to the outcome. It calls not only for a hearing ear but also an open mind and an understanding heart.

1. What might have contributed to Sue's fear?
    a. Natural timidity? If she feels, *Why should anyone listen to me?* she's in good company. Moses felt the same or worse; Genesis, Chapter 3, tells the story. Check especially vv. 10-12, then Chapter 4:10-12.
    b. Former experiences in being rejected when she has made a bid for forgiveness?
    c. A lack of knowledge, or failure to apply the Bible truths she does know?
    d. Any other factors?

2. How would you handle a situation such as Alma's where the outcome might have been physical damage to herself?

3. What did you learn from the behavior of the two ministers' wives?

4. How do you translate "Let not the sun go down on your anger" into your own everyday relationships, especially at home?

5. Imagine you have a problem like that of the estranged brothers. Ask yourself:
    a. How deeply does it trouble me?
    b. How willing am I to confess my part in it?
    c. How far am I willing to go—distance and attitude-wise—*by faith* alone, in an effort to restore the relationship?

6. What does Diane's, "Why should I be the one to forgive? say about the girl and her desire to please

the Lord?

7. How does Peggy betray her lack of faith? What is the risk in obeying the Lord's command to forgive?

8. The pros and cons of forgiveness by mail or telephone:

   a. Can you recount any negative experiences you have had?

   b. For the classic example of a successful written plea for forgiveness, read *The Living Bible* paraphrasing of Paul's letter to his friend Philemon (just 25 verses) for the runaway slave Onesimus, whose name means "useful." Paul writes, "He hasn't been of much use to you in the past . . . I am sending him back to you, and with him comes my own heart."

   What was the basis of Paul's expectations in writing to Philemon?

   How did he show his own unselfishness?

   What happy suggestion did he offer Philemon as a rationale for the slave's running away? What does this say to you about the Lord having *a plan for your life?*

   Note: You can read of Onesimus again. This time Paul calls him "a faithful and beloved brother who is one of you" (Col. 4:9).

   Are you saying, that's a beautiful story but it happened a long time ago? Or are you asking God to show you how, by letter or in person, you can put yourself on the line in order to intercede effectively for someone who needs to be forgiven and given a new start?

   How far will you go? And how soon?

CHAPTER 3

There's a kind of blasphemy in the blatant, "I can't forgive You, God."

As if God needed our forgiveness!

1. Under what circumstances have you been tempted to say (or think) "I can't forgive You, God"?

2. What can we learn of the character of God through His long-suffering toward us when we virtually throw His promises back in His face?

   How does David express this in Psalm 103:
   v. 8?
   v. 10?
   v. 14?
   other verses?

3. Why does it pay to let God *be* God in our lives?

4. What was Job's conclusion? (See Job 23:10.)

   How does Job's attitude and speech demonstrate unshakeable trust in God, whatever the outcome, in Job 13:15?

5. Since, by our behavior during a severe trial we influence onlookers to believe or disbelieve that God is sufficient for us, how should we pray at such times?

6. Psalm 46:10 (KJV) says, "Be still and know that I am God."

   What does "Be still" say to you? List several of your thoughts.

7. To the much-asked question, "Why *me?*" Job had the answer (Job 2:10). Explain what Job meant.

8. When evil comes into your life, do you dwell on it? Or does it cause you to think of how the good overbalances the bad?

9. *Focus* on the past week. Enumerate its blessings and then its misfortunes. Be honest and objective.

   Then, far from saying "I can't forgive You, God," stop and have a count-your-blessings, praise-to-God break.

CHAPTER 4

Christ spoke directly and forcefully on the issue of forgiveness. He knew all about it; He knew that He would give His life on a cross (like a common criminal) to make provision *for the sin of all mankind.*

1. There's enough forgiveness to go around.

   Read: John 3:16,17; 1 John 1:7, 2:2, 4:14; Romans 8:1,2.

   What does each verse mean to you?

   Memorize at least one of these verses which has a special meaning for you.

2. Forgiveness is a matter of the will. We determine *I will* or *I will not* forgive. God will not twist our arm or otherwise force us to seek and to extend forgiveness. But what are the spelled-out consequences when we "will not"? God will not honor such actions! (Matthew 6:15).

3. Think about the forgiveness you have extended to others. Would God be pleased with:

   a. the genuineness of your forgiveness?

   b. the manner in which you "forgive"?

   c. the strings you attach to it?

   d. the measurement?

4. How can we be sure that God, for Christ's sake, will indeed forgive us; then take it by faith?

   Why is it beneficial to us that we forgive the penitent?

   Is God bargaining with us in this matter of forgiveness?

5. Ask the Holy Spirit to show you where you have been stingy in forgiving and to help you become a generous forgiver.

   It won't be easy, but are you willing with the Holy Spirit's support, to go and confess, "I didn't really forgive you, and now I do want to"?

You can *be a great forgiver*, and with guaranteed results! Set a date now, and carry it through!

CHAPTER 5

The desire to "change" people is both human and understandable. But to make it a condition of their receiving our forgiveness is a wrong use of forgiveness.

Anyway, even if we do manage by some means to effect the change, we will doubtless find other reasons for withholding forgiveness—selfish reasons.

1. What if God would not forgive us until we reached a certain standard of acceptability? (Instead, we have the solid assurance of Ephesians 1:6 that we are "accepted in the beloved.")

2. Paul has something strong to say about sin's dominating us (Romans 6:12-14).

   How does Satan lure us to the point of his having dominion over us?

3. What would you consider to be a presumptuous sin (Psalm 19:13)?

4. What part can an impure motive play in unanswered prayer?

5. How, specifically, did the church fail Hal and Linda?

   When they stand before the Lord, how will their blaming this church for their spiritual downfall be viewed?

6. What can we learn, as witnesses for Christ, by the experiences of Eunice, and of David (the rock musician)?

7. According to Acts 1:8, what is the ultimate medium for change which God gives?

8. We see in 1 Corinthians 15:51 that "we shall all be changed." How ready are you—as a believer, as a witness for Christ—for that great coming change?

Ask yourself: If I could know that Christ was coming back tomorrow, what changes would I hasten to make?

CHAPTER 6

St. Augustine said, "The confession of evil works is the first beginning of good works."*

1. What is your definition of, and what is involved in *confession:*

   a. to God?
   b. to another person?
   c. to the church?

   Another use of the word *confess* is when we "confess with our mouth the Lord Jesus . . ." (Romans 10:9).

2. How would you differentiate between faults and sins?

3. Discuss:

   a. the pitfalls associated with confessing before the whole church;

   b. the potential harm to new believers or to any non-Christians present.

4. How would you as a member of the church in this chapter have accepted the recommendation that the erring pastor be given a second chance?

   a. What was the argument in his favor?

   b. What does this pastor still have to face up to—even though forgiveness has been given?

5. When confession takes place, what will best demonstrate that it is based on true repentance? (See Matthew 3:8, Acts 26:20.)

6. When Satan tempted Adam and Eve, what tactics did he use?

*p. 127, *Encyclopedia of Religious Quotations*—Frank S. Mead, Fleming H. Revell Company, 1976.

Which trait (that characterizes the serpent more than any other of God's creatures) undid Eve?

God has provided for us in even the most severe temptation. Memorize for such times 1 Corinthians 10:13; also, James 4:7.

7. Contrast David's condition *following* his confession of sins (Psalm 32:1,2) with his state *before* he confessed (vv. 3,4).

8. What does the fear of Joseph's brothers that they would still be punished for their earlier treatment of him reveal about them?

   How do you deal with guilt feelings based on incidents long past?

9. If someone were honestly defending you as a "sample" of Christian behavior, what fruits would they be able to hold up as exhibits?

   This is a good moment to ask the Holy Spirit to reveal to you how you need to change in order to be a credible Christian.

CHAPTER 7

It's exciting to realize that through everyday experiences God will teach us, giving us new, fresh insights that can enrich our own lives and improve our relationships with other people.

1. How does forgiveness equate with excusing?

   a. At what point (if any) are we justified in becoming angry at someone?

   b. How can we handle such anger in a scriptural manner (Ephesians 4:26)? This is a whole area by itself. It helps when we turn the anger over to the Lord. It's not the person, but the person's *behavior* which causes the anger.

2. In what way do we set standards for other people to live up to?

   a. What are we presuming when we impose our

expectations upon them?

   b. How would you help a friend to understand that he is out of line, that it's not his business, not his responsibility to legislate how you or someone else lives?

3. What part does asking forgiveness play when the other person sets himself up (unknowingly, perhaps) as your judge?

4. How can you make Micah 6:8 more true in your life through:

   a. doing justly?
   b. loving mercy?
   c. walking humbly with God?

Where does all the strength, patience, wisdom, love and long-suffering needed to obey *God's standard* come from?

5. What was behind the mother-in-law's unwillingness to believe that God had changed her son-in-law?

How did this bad attitude work for good in the new convert's case?

6. Think of a time when you asked God to "enter a *C* for cancel."

Did you wonder:

If the computer was "down"?

If your sin was too big to be cancelled?

If God would believe you meant it when you sought His forgiveness?

If the guilt of your sin would reappear after having been blotted out?

If guilt reappears, what do you need to remember?

7. In the light of God's dealing with our sins—blotting out the record against us—how should we treat other people? (They have sinned against us; they have repented and made restitution where called for; and we have "forgiven" them.)

146

a. What about the file drawer of your mind? Does it contain memory garbage?

b. How willing are you to ask the Holy Spirit—and mean it—to enable you to forget?

c. On the practical side, what "evidence" are you hoarding that needs to be totally destroyed? Today is the only day you can be sure of. Decide "Today is take-out-the-garbage day."

d. The last word is *do it now*—and know a new peace of heart.

CHAPTER 8

Insistence on being right all the time is a childish trait. For many people it's a long road to maturity, the place where you can let the other person "be right."

For those of you who have to live with—or are, yourself—a compulsive "I'm right" person, there is help. It need not be a forever situation.

1. What could cause a person to have a need to be proven right?

2. How is this being-right-all-the-time syndrome akin to childish behavior, whatever the person's age?

3. How do you personally react to such people with their "You're wrong, I'm right" spirit?

   a. Does it make you stop and think?

   b. Do you suggest you talk it over?

   c. Do you get *mad?*

   d. How do you think the "soft answer" of Proverbs 15:1 fits in here?

4. When something is at issue, when it is important to be right and to say so, how would you *word* your feelings? Where would you place the emphasis?

5. In what ways does Mr. Always Right damage his Christian witness? How would you interpret Peter Marshall's statement?

6. Of what good things are the "always right" robbing themselves?

Consider how they miss:

a. the blessing of God (James 4:6);

b. growth as loving Christians (1 Corinthians 13:4);

c. friends (Proverbs 15:12,14,18).

7. Jesus is the only one who ever lived who could truthfully, unequivocably have said at all times, "I am right."

Question yourself: How often, in the course of talking about something I feel very strongly about, do I stop and ponder, "What would Jesus say? How would He say it?"

8. With so many who still have not heard the Gospel, right now I'm asking the Holy Spirit to:

a. control my thoughts

b. help me become more sensitive toward the one I'm witnessing to

c. guard my tongue

CHAPTER 9

In the matter of forgiveness (as in all else) we cannot always trust our own heart. Why? Jeremiah spells it out for us:

"The heart is more deceitful than all else and desperately sick, who can understand it?" (Jeremiah 17:9).

1. There's an obvious flaw in the "forgiveness" Margaret dishes out. How would such easy forgiveness leave you feeling?

2. Why is partial or "handle-sticking-up" forgiveness a mockery of the word?

a. Think of the extent of Christ's forgiveness.

b. What if He had partially or conditionally forgiven us?

c. What does His prayer on the Cross (Luke 23:34) say to you? How much does it move you?

3. In the context of forgiveness, how would you translate this Scripture into your own life?

   "I tell you this: there is not a thoughtless word that comes from men's lips but they will have to account for it on the day of judgment" (Matthew 12:36 NEB).

4. In the mother-in-law dilemma, how did each of the following determine the happy ending?
   a. Her admission of helplessness and need of God's wisdom:
   b. Her prayer and heart-searching:
   c. Her willingness to listen to the voice of God:
   d. Her obedience in activating God's counsel:

5. Why is a "soft answer" (Proverb 25:15) often the simplest, surest solution?

   What examples can you cite from your own experience of when:
   a. you did give a soft answer?
   b. you "gave as good as you got"?

6. What is your reaction to:
   a. the conference speaker's prayer that she forget as well as forgive?
   b. her remembering where and when she "forgot"?

   How do you relate this to Paul's "forgetting those things which are behind?" (Philippians 3:13).

8. What are several reasons why Miriam's friends and her church ought to have supported and encouraged her following her repentance and restoration?

9. Rate yourself:

   Where do I fit in, in the examples cited in this chapter?

   What kind of "forgiver" am I, really?

What changes will I begin to make to be more like Jesus?

CHAPTER 10

The first instance of jealousy in action was Satan's attempt to come between God and Adam and Eve. We know only too well the dire outcome.

The first murder in human history doubtless can be attributed to jealousy and its first cousin, envy (Genesis 4:3-8), when Cain killed his brother Abel. Ever since, these evils have plagued the human race.

1. Study the various situations in this chapter. Discuss the specific outworking of a jealous spirit and the effects this had on each of the people involved.

2. List several ways jealousy might manifest itself in your life.

3. What, in your opinion, could be some causes of jealousy?

4. Think of an instance when you have been the victim of someone's jealousy. Think of an instance when you have been jealous of someone else.

5. What price does the jealous person pay for allowing himself to give vent to feelings of jealousy?

6. In all the Bible, with its constant emphasis on the love of God, we read of only seven things which God hates (Proverb 6:16-19). Read these verses and list all the links to jealousy that you can find.

7. Solomon questions, "Who is able to stand before envy?" (Proverb 27:4). How would you refute the despair of such a question?

You can't by yourself uproot the weeds in your life.

How willing are you to begin today to pray diligently, to evaluate your feelings honestly, and then confess to any whom you have hurt by your jealousy? Above all, how will you daily *seek the moment-by-moment help of the Holy Spirit* in your relationsips?

CHAPTER 11

We can reasonably assume that at one time or another everyone falls into at least one of these three categories:

"I can't forgive (someone else)"

"I can't forgive God"

"I can't forgive myself"

Some unhappy persons rob themselves of the peace that God is ready to give them by falling prey to all three.

1. As you have read this chapter, what reactions/ emotions have you found characterizing the individuals in the illustrations?

2. In what way do these characteristics (and others like them):

   a. displease God?

   b. refute His promises? (Romans 5:1).

   What part does an individual's lack of faith play? (See Hebrews 11:6.)

3. Discuss the six areas that contribute to: "I can't forgive myself."

   a. The inability to forget.

   b. The felt need for punishment.

   c. The fact that guilt feelings may be more tolerable than relentless remorse.

   d. The inability to accept *by faith* that God's forgiveness is limitless.

   e. A distorted sense of humility.

   f. A lack of demonstrated forgiveness from others on earlier occasions.

4. God does not reckon sins as great-greater-greatest. On what score did Paul declare himself to be "the chief of sinners"?

   Why was Paul able to forgive himself and go on from being Saul the persecutor to Paul the apostle? (See

1 Timothy 1:12-16.)

In what sense did Paul consider himself "Exhibit A" (v. 16)?

5. What can you relate to in Peter's life?

   In what ways have you denied the Lord Jesus Christ?

   Having repented and confessed, what causes you to *know* that He has forgiven you?

6. How much stock can you place in the statement, "Don't hold yourself responsible for what you cannot control"?

7. Under what circumstances (if ever) have you felt or said, "I can't forgive myself"?

   What helped you most to see the folly of your attitude?

8. The basis of all forgiveness is that "God, for Christ's sake, has forgiven us" (Ephesians 4:32 KJV). If you can't forgive yourself, ask:

   a. On what am I basing *my* inability to forgive myself?

   b. What am I going to do about what *God* has said?

      Psalm 86:4-7—for your day of trouble:
      Psalm 103:10-13—His great lovingkindness:
      Matthew 9:2—offering courage:
      Matthew 11:28—a divine burden bearer:
      1 John 1:9—full forgiveness:
      1 John 2:12—the guarantee:

   With these, and a host of kindred verses of assurance, how will you take a positive step away from your inability to forgive yourself and begin to affirm that God loves you and that you believe the Bible?

CHAPTER 12

If we're honest, most of us will admit to being to some degree "forgiveness scorekeepers."

Even so, doesn't it seem incredible that Peter, companion and eyewitness of Christ's compassion and willingness to forgive, should be number-conscious when it came to extending forgiveness?

1. On what am I basing my confidence that God will forgive me?

   Scripture verses:

2. Why, on the basis of our own forgiveness by God, can we be assured we will never run out of our quota of being forgiven?

3. What does our keeping score reveal about us?

4. What effect have negative reactions to your honest attempts at reconciliation had upon you?

   What can you learn in this regard from Amy Carmichael?

5. What does Psalm 103:10 say to you?

   Cite an example from your own experience of God's "not keeping score."

6. Which Bible verses, when they penetrated the long hardened heart of the 80-year-old Josh, gave him hope of deliverance from sin and acceptance from God?

   a. *Isaiah:*
      Hebrews:

   b. Which others would you have "prescribed" for his case?

7. How did this elderly convert prove he was repentant? By what power did his wife retain her faith and ability to be a living testimony in a hard place?

8. Will you invite the Holy Spirit to bring to your mind someone whom you have given up on? Who, in your thinking, has sinned away his last chance? With the heaped up evidence that God forgets the number of times you come asking for forgiveness, when will you now go to that person in faith with your offer of full forgiveness?

CHAPTER 13

Have you considered that it's in our own best interests that we obey God's decree to be forgiving?

Take Sam, the atheist who actually brags that he will never forgive anyone. At the judgment seat, unless he has a change of heart and repents, his forgiveness debts will catch up with him.

1. Lillian admits to suffering physically and is helped to relate her symptoms to an unpaid debt of forgiveness. (See 3 John:2.)

   a. How do the attitudes and resolutions of Sam and Lillian differ?

   b. How much does Lillian save? (What is the going price of holding a grudge? of severed fellowship with God?)

2. Analyze Lillian's motive in extending forgiveness.

   What gave her confidence that God would help her in her resolve to pay her debt?

3. How justified was Steve in his criticism of church members?

   To what extent and in what ways is a church member responsible for the church's credibility in the community?

   a. Whose church is it (Colossians 1:18, Matthew 16:18)?

b. What did the church cost (Ephesians 5:25, Colossians 1:24)?

4. What price does the church pay when:
   a. a member is disloyal and does not reflect the true image?
   b. there is a dearth of earnest prayer?
   c. there is squabbling and dissent?

5. What extra blessing did Mildred merit by taking the initiative in seeking reconciliation with her friend (Matthew 5:9)?

6. What will it cost to ensure "good thought" input (Philippians 4:8)?

   What form of discipline prevents pollution of the mind (Colossians 3:2)?

7. How much does pride like Phyllis's and honesty like Carla's cost a Christian? What counsel would you offer them from your experience?

8. Ask yourself:

   What do *I* consider too high a price to pay for withholding forgiveness?

   How credible an example am I?

   How am I:
      enhancing the church?
      hindering the church?

   How sure am I that I have, as far as I can determine, no outstanding forgiveness debts for which I will pay the high price?

CHAPTER 14

How often do you hear, or say yourself, "I'd like to... but I just can't afford it?" (Meanwhile, we spend for some things we may be able to do without.)

Two things we can afford: to love, and to forgive.

We love Him because He first loved us (1 John 4:19).

We forgive because first we are forgiven.

1. Can we separate love and forgiveness? Contrast:
   a. the woman with the alabaster box (Luke 7:36-49);
   b. the unmerciful servant (Matthew 18:23-35).

   Notice that they are *both* "immortalized." What did they have in common?

2. What would you say is the most important reason the Bible records so many facets of David's life?

   If you had been David, how likely is it that you would have returned Saul's hatred with love for Saul's family and a desire to help them?

3. Matthew 5:11 promises a special blessing for those who are reviled. What is the special reason for this blessing?

   Why should we, as followers of Jesus Christ, expect to suffer persecution? (See John 16:33, 2 Timothy 3:12.)

4. Forgiveness is not something we should store up. Forgiveness debts, like any others, can create added problems; we have to pay "interest." What are some of those added problems?

5. The Holy Spirit delights in enabling us. We will never come to Him once too often and hence be turned away. Once we realize that forgiving is not a do-it-yourself matter, we never need let interest mount up. We'll be well able to afford to forgive.

   Ask yourself:
   a. What interest debt am I allowing to play havoc with my relationships?
   b. How long do I intend to let the interest accrue?
   c. When will I confess my unforgiveness to the Lord, seek the Holy Spirit's strength and assurance that He will be with me, then *do whatever it takes?* (It will not be you, but *Christ in your* who emboldens you to clear that forgiveness debt.)

TEN STEPS TO FREEDOM
THROUGH FORGIVENESS

1. Keep praising God that, for Christ's sake, He has forgiven you.

2. *Believe* that you are truly forgiven. (You can't trust your *feelings!*)

3. Keep a short account: confess the sin, accept God's forgiveness, and close that account.

4. Reinforce your certainty by memorizing strong "forgiveness" verses in the Bible: Psalm 86:5, Psalm 103:12, Colossians 1:14, 1 John 1:9.

5. Pray for deliverance from deliberate and hidden sin (Psalm 19:12,13; 1 Corinthians 10:15).

6. Remember what your "free" forgiveness cost the Son of God. Don't be a repeater. Having been forgiven, claim victory over that sin through the power of the Holy Spirit within you.

7. Pray for the person whom you need to forgive.

8. Be a generous forgiver—freely you received, freely pass it on.

9. Refuse to let your mind dwell on something you've forgiven.

10. Forgive yourself. Rather than wallow in debilitating, fruitless regrets, glory in the freedom that is yours through God's forgiveness.

—Jeanette Lockerbie

Here is a little chart that you can cut out if you like and paste in the back of your Bible. It will remind you of the helpful steps toward a life of freedom through continual forgiveness.